Disciples and Leaders

THE ORIGINS OF CHRISTIAN MINISTRY IN THE NEW TESTAMENT

John F. O'Grady

Paulist Press
New York/Mahwah

Library of Congress Cataloging-in-Publication Data

O'Grady, John F.
    Disciples and leaders: the origins of Christian ministry in the New Testament/John F. O'Grady.
        p.   cm.
    Includes bibliographical references.
    ISBN 0-8091-3269-9
    1. Clergy—Office—Biblical teaching. 2. Jesus Christ—Views on ministry. 3. Apostles—Biblical teaching. 4. Church—Biblical teaching. 5. Peter, the Apostle, Saint. 6. Service (Theology)—Biblical teaching. 7. Catholic Church—Clergy. 8. Catholic Church—Doctrines. I. Title. II. Title: Ministry in the New Testament.
BS2545.C56047   1991
262'.1—dc20   91-27034
                                                              CIP

Published by Paulist Press
997 Macarthur Boulevard
Mahwah, New Jersey 07430

Printed and bound in the
United States of America

Contents

I do not cease to give thanks for you in my prayers that the God of our Lord Jesus Christ, the Father of glory, may give you a spirit of wisdom and of revelation in the knowledge of him, having the eyes of your hearts enlightened, that you may know the hope to which he has called you, what are the riches of his glorious inheritance in the saints . . .

Ephesians 1:16–18

———————

For Laura Suarez Armesto

Michael Joseph Griffin and Joseph Patrick Lee

and

The Barry University Community

Preface

The meaning of ministry within the Christian church always needs further study. Actual ministry, however, takes place in spite of all the scrutiny. Orthopraxis makes Christianity credible rather than orthodoxy. For two thousand years people have accepted belief in Jesus and his church and have attempted to live lives based upon the gospel. Who knows the careful details of their beliefs? They lived their lives on the simple call to love the brethren, to seek to overcome evil, to offer forgiveness and in many cases to give their lives for others. Many would probably fail a detailed theological examination of the understanding of their faith. No one even tried to demand such an examination. As long as Jesus was accepted and believers tried their best to live according to his teaching and example, the church flourished.

I know that ministry makes sense only when people minister to each other. People have to take care of people; those in need have to depend upon those who can help. Those who can help must do so. I also know that this book may have little effect on the millions of Christians who go about their lives doing good. They do not need to study the origins of Christian ministry. They live it.

This book, however, does try to respond to a felt need. Any organized religion can become formalized. A single tradition can crowd out other equally good and valid traditions. Every so often those who are leaders, those who teach and even those who are actively engaged in ministry have to return to the roots. Such an enterprise not only gives new support for current church activities, but also allows an evaluation of structures or procedures based on the ministry of Jesus and his early communities.

In my adult life I have enjoyed the leisure to study the New Testament, and in particular the gospels. I have also had both an interest and opportunity to study both new Testament christology and the history of christology, especially the thought of contemporary theologians.

While a graduate student I had the good pleasure to attend the lectures of Karl Rahner, S.J. on "The Event and Means of Salvation." That experience continues to influence my thought on Jesus, the church and ministry. Here I acknowledge my indebtedness to that great twentieth century theologian. Like many other of my contemporaries, the thought of Karl Rahner has radically transformed my ideas on Christianity.

I remember a comment made by my mother which fits well this relationship between ordinary people of faith and theologians. I had recently been ordained and my mother asked me about limbo. I told her that limbo was a teaching that appears only in an indirect way in two church documents and that the concept arose in a dispute in the seventeenth century. I also informed her of the joke that limbo was evacuated at the Second Vatican Council. Her response: "I never believed in it anyway. I could never accept a God who would condemn an innocent baby to live forever apart from God. I listened when the priests told me about limbo, and I never said anything but I never believed it."

Theologians, popes, bishops, priests and religious can say what they want. People of faith will still make up their own minds on how they relate to God and what God and his Christ mean to them. This book may have much to say about Jesus, the church, the New Testament, and ministry. No matter.

Faithful people will continue to live a life based on their understanding of Jesus, and they will make this world a better place because they have lived.

As always, I am indebted to many who have helped me in my education, in my efforts to clarify my thoughts, and in the actual production of this book. I have already mentioned Karl Rahner. Raymond Brown, S.S. has helped me to understand more accurately the New Testament. I hope that this work will add to that understanding for others.

Students continue to teach me by their questions and their reactions. I am particularly grateful to the graduate students in theology at Barry University in the years 1987–1990. Often they challenged me and forced me to rethink and reformulate and even seek more understandable expressions of my thought. To all of them, I offer my gratitude.

Dr. Laura Armesto of the English department and Dr. Mary Ann Jungbauer of the chemistry department and Dr. J. Patrick Lee, vice-president of academic affairs, each read the manuscript and helped me in making it more readable and more accurate in American English usage. I offer them my gratitude as well.

Finally, I must acknowledge the support of the Barry University community. The three years I have been here I consider a blessing. Administration, faculty, staff and students form a caring community. I am richer through their presence.

The example of thousands of others who have ministered to me in my lifetime encourages me to write this book. I hope that it will encourage those in ministry to persevere and invite others to join in Christian service.

Miami, 1990

CHAPTER 1

Faith Statements on Jesus and the Church

Theology flourishes on faith statements. Throughout the centuries men and women of faith have developed simple, clear expressions of faith, and on these faith statements theologians have built their systems of explanations. The Bible offers a treasure trove of faith statements, from: "So God created man in his own image, in the image of God he created him" (Gen 1:27), to: "He [Jesus] is the image of the invisible God" (Col 1:15). Each statement becomes part of the religious heritage. The first expresses the fundamental understanding of human dignity in Judaism. The same faith statement becomes part of the Christian heritage and is joined with the second: Jesus is related to God, and Jesus is also the image of God as all people form this likeness. People must freely accept the faith statement, for no one can prove its validity. No middle ground exists in faith statements. Individuals accept or reject. Often enough, many of these faith statements in Christianity express the presuppositions that form part of the Christian tradition. We can never completely analyze them, nor can we completely explain them. They exist as part of the meaning of Christianity.

Over the centuries from the time of the writings of the New Testament many individual believers struggled with the many faith statements to try to convey their meaning. They used stories, other images, abstract and concrete language to try

1

to hand on from one generation to another the fundamental idea contained in the basic faith statements. The content of the faith statement always remained more important than the images or language used by the believers. With the passage of time, the church adapted these faith statements to new situations. Something remained the same, and something developed.

"Jesus is God's gift to the human race through the power of God" is a faith statement that emphasizes the gratuity of the presence of Jesus in human history as an expression of love. The faith statement also offers the source for Jesus as part of the human race: the power of God. This faith statement takes on a fuller expression in the gospels of Matthew and Luke as they present the origin of Jesus in their infancy narratives. Paul teaches a similar doctrine in his great hymns to the wonder of God in giving us Jesus:

> For I am sure that neither death, nor life nor angels nor principalities, nor things present nor things to come, nor powers nor height, nor depth, nor anything else in all creation will be able to separate us from the love of God in Christ Jesus our Lord (Rom 8:38–39).

"God raised up Jesus of Nazareth" (Acts 2:24). "Christ is the power of God" (1 Cor 1:24). These faith statements express succinctly that God's power would not permit Jesus to be overcome in death by the power of darkness and evil. The power of goodness in God destroys death for Jesus and raises him to make him both Lord and Christ (Acts 2:36). In the oft-quoted words of Karl Barth: the crucifixion of Jesus was humanity's no and the resurrection was God's yes.[1]

The various writers of the New Testament have offered many faith statements about the church as well as about Jesus: "You are Peter and upon this rock I will build my church, and the gates of hell shall not prevail against it" (Mt 16:18); "Christ is the head of the church" (Eph 5:23); "He [Christ] is the head of the body, the church" (Col 1:18). During the two thousand years of Christianity, theologians and church councils have added their own faith statements to those of the New Testament about Jesus and his church. Each faith statement offers some understanding of the meaning of Jesus and Christianity and at the same time leaves the believer ever open to a fuller understanding.

This work examines certain faith statements about Jesus and his church, paying particular attention to the origin of Christian ministry. No final answer to the many questions facing ministry today can be given in this study. Rather, through the examination of the New Testament, the reader will learn of the complexity of the issue when we treat the origin and meaning of Jesus and the origin and meaning of Christian ministry.

We begin with a study of the entrance of Jesus into history and the resurrection of Jesus, by which he passes out of history. Both involve the power of God. Without God and his goodness we would not have Jesus as part of the history of the human race, and without that same power and goodness we would not have Jesus as Lord and Christ. Because God is God, no human can ask whether or not God needed to give us Jesus. God is the foundation of freedom and rights. God freely gave the human race a Lord and Christ in Jesus. Christian faith affirms these faith statements, for faith accepts Jesus as God's gift and as the Lord and Christ of the human race and of all creation. The presence of the Christian church in human history also manifests the power and goodness of God. God sustains this church through his Spirit. The one God gave Jesus to humanity as Lord and continues to give to humanity the ongoing ministry of this Lord through the church.

The ministry of Jesus fulfilled his commitment to God his

Father. He preached the reign of God. He shared in the authority of God and exercised a ministry of power. Jesus overcame evil, forgave sins, changed people's hearts. Jesus was a prophet in deed as well as in word. During this same ministry he called others to share in his ministry. He gave them authority and power and made disciples and called apostles. After his resurrection, these same followers continued the ministry of Jesus through the presence of his Spirit. The power of God gave birth to the church, and the church continues the same ministry of Jesus throughout the ages. What Jesus had received from God, he handed on to his early followers, and they in turn created a church to continue the ministry of Jesus begun by the power of God.

At this juncture in history, Christians have centuries of experience with church ministry along with the exercise of authority and power in the church. Some of that history seems far from the ministry of Jesus. Much of it gives clear evidence of a ministry similar to that of Jesus flourishing in the lives of countless men and women of great faith. History, however, holds on to the best and the worst. Those who study it may point with pride to how much the ministry of Jesus has contributed to the changing face of this earth. These same students of history also may acknowledge with pain how those committed to this ministry have frequently failed. The church as an institution has contributed both negatively and positively to the human family. By far the goodness has outweighed the negative contribution. A constant return to the sources always helps in increasing the positive and decreasing the negative.

This book is written from a particular perspective with a particular purpose in mind. The New Testament is normative for Christianity. The church of every age must return continually to its roots and submit itself to the scrutiny of that sacred book which expresses in written form the religious experience of Jesus and his early followers. Contemporary ministry within the church for its members and without the church for those who share a common humanity will find its foundation on the continuation of the ministry of Jesus through his Spirit. Christian ministry is powerful. Christians still try to overcome evil in themselves, in others, and in the world around them. Christians continue to forgive sins. People's hearts are inflamed and their lives are changed when they encounter the power of God for goodness in all who claim to follow the example of Jesus of Nazareth. For almost two thousand years, men and women of faith have continued this same ministry and the world continues to be enriched by their presence. The reality of failure in ministry can never destroy the positive contributions just as the evil that caused the death of Jesus could never destroy him. God does not allow evil to overcome goodness.

Jesus and the church are inseparable. We can better understand Jesus when we see how he gathered a community around himself. We can understand the church as the continuation of this community when we return frequently to what Jesus did, what he taught and how he fulfilled his ministry. No one can ever separate Jesus from the church and vice versa. Nor can anyone separate Jesus and the church from the testimony that forms the New Testament. If some people lay claim to be followers of the Lord and do not join with other followers in the church, they are not true followers of Jesus. If others lay claim to be members of the church without constantly measuring that church by the standards of the ministry of Jesus, they too are not members of the church of Jesus. If anyone claims to be both a follower of Jesus and part of the church and does not constantly place both self and church under the scrutiny of the light of the New Testament, that person has lost the roots that make Christianity stable and true.

Theology always exists as incomplete and imperfect. The human effort to understand faith always falls short. Even the New Testament itself fails to convey in any complete sense the meaning of Jesus. Theologians and people of faith must constantly seek a renewal of understanding by returning to roots and applying and using any knowledge that can further unfold the meaning of those roots.

In this book I will try to present Jesus and the church as understood in the New Testament with particular emphasis on the ministry of Jesus and on how this ministry continues in the church. I will also pay attention to how this ministry originated and to how both Jesus and his followers exercised that ministry. If we can better appreciate the origins of Christian ministry, we can better evaluate contemporary ministry. The New Testament supports much of what Christians do, but not everything. The New Testament also encourages these same Christians to evaluate what they do. Then Christians may make whatever changes they deem necessary to assure the continuation of the ministry of Jesus: what he did and said and how he ministered to others.

In an earlier article[2] I attempted to explain some contemporary thoughts on authority and power and to apply them to the understanding of contemporary church issues. Here I will simply recall some of those ideas.

Ministry, whether of Jesus or of the church, demands some authority,[3] a right to influence[4] people's lives, their thoughts and their behavior. Ministry also demands the ability or the power[5] to accomplish its expectations. Jesus had both right and power. The church has both right and power. Authority or right can be exercised because of some absolute title or position. It can rest upon law or learning, and finally the right or authority can flow from the inner depths of the person. This last type of authority we call charismatic. Jesus might have claimed the absolute authority of God but he did not. He might have claimed the authority of the law or learning, but he chose not to do so. Jesus exercised a charismatic authority in his ministry.[6]

Power can be positive or negative. Power can exploit or manipulate. Power can cause competition or it can be supportive and nurturing. Finally power can be persuasive and integrative, recognizing the power of the other.[7] Jesus never exploited. His manipulation was positive; he seems to have disliked competitive power and he was frequently nurturing. Finally Jesus in his ministry never imposed. He let people decide to accept or reject him and his gospel. In the gospel of John when the author recounts the teaching on the eucharist as the bread of life, Jesus asks: "Will you also go away?" (Jn 6:67). People need not stay unless they choose.

The church has no choice but to follow the example of Jesus in its ministry. Charismatic men and women have always been part of the history of Christianity. People of learning in spirituality and theology spring up in every period of Christian history. Ministry frequently demands nurturing. It may even utilize some manipulation, but ministry always allows the individual to be free to decide for or against.

How the church will function in the twenty-first century depends on the demands of the new era. Always, however, the ministry of the Christian church must continue the example of the one Lord who came "not to be served but to serve and to give his life as a ransom for many" (Mk 10:45).

We begin with faith statements associated with the origin of Jesus. There the power of God becomes manifest. God shows us a sign of the greatest power in the resurrection. We must also study the origin and meaning of the risen Lord and how the early Christians formulated their faith in Jesus, who was made both Lord and Christ (Acts 2:36). The rest of this work will deal with ministry: that of Jesus and the early church. The work concludes with the development of the hierarchical church.

It matters little what form the church organization will take in the future provided that all is based on the life, ministry, death and resurrection of Jesus of Nazareth whom God has made Lord of all. Faith statements will continue to develop as men and women of faith continue the age-old search for applying the gospel to ever new situations. Ultimately, however, all that really counts is the firm belief that God has given us both Jesus and the church.

CHAPTER 2

The Origin of Jesus

Historians verify events which fall within space and time. They also must have some point of comparison within ordinary human experience. Thus historians have trouble with the miraculous. The verification which seems easy to many human experiences often eludes even the most careful examination when the historian must face an event which does not fit into space and time and which goes beyond the normal activity of human life. The miraculous always causes problems.

In Christian tradition the virginal conception, or the entrance of Jesus into history, carries with it an important miraculous element. Both Matthew and Luke explain the origin of Jesus by involving the power of God. Historians at the time of Jesus could deal with a fertilized ovum in a woman's womb if they had a way to verify this scientifically but could not deal with a fertilized ovum if the origin was unknown, or beyond the ordinary mode of human reproduction.

If we accept the traditional teaching about conception, then we can say that the life of Jesus in history extended from the first moment of his conception in the Virgin Mary to his last breath on the cross when he died. His entrance into history is associated with the virginal conception, and his exit from history is associated with his death and glorification in the resurrection. How he entered into our history and how he left history in his resurrection leaves much to the unknown. God the Father is the principal actor: God sends his Son, the Word, and the Word becomes flesh in a woman. God glorifies this

Son in the resurrection. The Word pre-existed the coming into human history and continues to exist in the glorified Jesus after his death. Only people of faith recognized the coming of the Word of God into history and only people of faith recognized the resurrected Jesus. Jesus as a gift of God to the human race through the power of God is a faith statement. Jesus made Lord and Christ in his resurrection by the power of God is also a faith statement.

Over the past twenty years much has been written on the virginal conception[1] and on the resurrection of the Lord.[2] But even with the frequent exchange of ideas, many questions remain unanswered and many problems remain unsolved. Most believers will be content to affirm belief in the virginal conception and in the bodily resurrection and leave it at that. Others, however, will continue the pursuit: faith seeking understanding even if such a quest continues to stir controversy.

Every theologian must write as a member of the believing community. Theologians explore with the tools of exegesis and theological methodology the data surrounding articles of faith with their implications and limitations. I do not propose to resolve the many issues associated with the virginal conception and bodily resurrection of the Lord. I propose, however, to review the ideas involved in an effort to explain where we have been and in what direction we seem to be moving. By this approach not only will the task of theology continue, but those who are interested will begin to understand the dilemmas in which theologians often find themselves. We will come to a better understanding of Jesus and of his ministry if we have some understanding of his human origins and of his becoming Lord and Christ in his resurrection. We will also understand the ministry of the church better if we root this ministry in the power of God which gave us Christ and the power of God which raised up Christ as Lord and savior.

This chapter will be devoted to the entrance of Jesus into

human history. The following chapter will treat the meaning of the risen Lord as one who enables his followers to continue his ministry through the power of his Spirit. Only after the disciples had come to accept Jesus as risen Lord could they understand his ministry and, in fact, also understand his origins.

THE ENTRANCE OF THE WORD OF GOD INTO HISTORY

The virginal conception is primarily christological and not mariological. In the past some theologians concentrated on the role of Mary and the meaning of the entrance of Jesus into history for his mother. Certainly the event has great mariological significance but it concerns the conception and the birth of an individual, Jesus of Nazareth, and should be viewed primarily from the part of the Word's entrance into history rather than from the perspective of Mary in this entrance. Jesus as the one who preached the reign of God needed human origins and needed a special relationship to God if he was to fulfill his destiny. The emphasis must always fall on Jesus, however, and then on those whom God chose to participate in this event in history. Certain foundational statements may prove helpful. From the New Testament we can draw some definite conclusions:

1. His mother's name was Mary.
2. Many thought that his father was Joseph.
3. Many believed his birth had significance for all people.
4. He was probably born early, within the nine-month period after Joseph and Mary had begun to live together.

5. His grandfather's name was Jacob.
6. The writers of the gospels of Matthew and Luke attributed the origin of Jesus to the power of God.

Of the six statements above, an historian can verify the first five. The final statement is a faith statement beyond the power of verification other than a belief based on the acceptance of God and the power of God.

All of these statements, however, come to us from the gospels and not from the earliest witnesses of the New Testament. Paul, first in Galatians and then in Romans, offers the earliest witness to the origin of Jesus:

> But when the time had fully come, God sent forth his Son,
> born of a woman, born under the law, to redeem those
> under the law (Gal 4:4–5).

In this statement Paul is not primarily interested in the origin of Jesus. He is dealing with a pastoral problem on the relationship between Judaism and the law and Christianity. He roots Jesus in the human race (born of a woman) and then in the tradition of Judaism (born under the law). Then, however, he wishes to go beyond Judaism by claiming that he has come to "redeem those under the law." Such is his primary concern. We can also conclude that for Paul the origin of Jesus takes place in history at a particular time and place, that the principal actor is God who sent his Son, that like all other humans he was born of woman, and that he was a Jew. His birth had significance for the Jews, for he was to redeem those under the law. In his ministry Paul will claim that Jesus also has significance for Gentiles. Paul makes no mention of a virginal conception. Jesus was human and Jewish and had an unusual relationship with God: he was God's Son. Whether this implies pre-existence or not is unknown. Recently R. Fuller has argued effectively that not only has this verse nothing to do with the virginal conception, but it also does not involve any sense of pre-existence nor the sending of wisdom.[3] With regard to ministry the statement implies that Jesus was part of the human family and part of a particular religious tradition. Jesus directed his ministry to redeem people living under the law. Paul will go beyond that ministry of Jesus to extend the gospel to all.

> The gospel concerning his Son, who was descended from David according to the flesh (*sarx*) and designated Son of God in power according to the spirit (*pneuma*) of holiness by his resurrection from the dead (Rom 1:3–4).

Once again Paul designates Jesus as human and Jewish: he was descended from David. Here, however, he does not emphasize the coming of the Son of God into human history through the sending by God the Father, but the designation of Jesus as Son in power. He also speaks not of the Holy Spirit (a term used by Matthew and Luke) but of the spirit of holiness. Because Jesus possesses holiness, because he is close to God, he becomes the Son in power in his resurrection from the dead. This spirit of holiness brings the resurrection and forms the foundation of Christian ministry as it founded the ministry of Jesus.

By this time in his life Paul had suffered the failure of his Gentile ministry in Antioch,[4] so that when he wrote to the Christian community at Rome he wished to modify some of his previous positions. Paul is willing to compromise, but he will not lose sight of his fundamental understanding of Jesus as Son of God in power. Paul admits the Jewish origins of Jesus but will not remain on that level. Now Jesus has gone beyond his Jewish traditions. As Son of God in power, Jesus can give his spirit to anyone who will receive it. For Paul's ministry, that means the Gentiles.

The use of the Greek word *sarx* (flesh) denotes human origin and the earthly form of life. The reference to David specifies his tradition. Spirit (*pneuma*) denotes his mode of living after the resurrection. Son of God in power also stresses this new way of existing, as does his reference to the resurrection. Jesus experienced an earthly existence and now experiences another form of existence through his resurrection. We do not have here an ontology, however, but rather a history of salvation: previously he had lived an earthly life and now he lives a life as Son of God in power. On this basis Paul can preach his gospel of freedom from the law for all, Jew and Gentile.

New Testament scholars[5] accept these earliest witnesses to the origin of Jesus as pre-Pauline. They existed in the Christian community and Paul appropriated them to suit his purpose in writing to both Galatians and Romans. The general meaning connoted by the texts focuses on a prophetic-sending-of-the-Son christology. The early Christian community attributed to Jesus a double identity, Son of David and Son of God, and applied this to the resurrection of Jesus. The authors of the infancy narratives then applied this christology to the virginal conception. These faith formulations recognized the humanness of Jesus and his Jewish heritage. Moreover, the first hints at a special relationship to God, and the second specifies this relationship as Son of God in power through the resurrection. Eventually this post-resurrection theology will contend that Jesus was God's Son through the power of the Spirit from the first moment of his conception. While the authors of the infancy accounts deal with his conception, the emphasis remains on what he became and accomplished through the power of God rather than on who he was. Functional christology predates an ontological christology.[6]

We should also consider Philippians 2:6–8:

Who, though he was in the form of God,
did not count equality with God a thing to be grasped,
but emptied himself,
taking the form of a servant,
being born in the likeness of men.

Although attributed to Paul, this hymn predates the epistle[7] and presents the Christ story in three movements: pre-
existence, existence and post-existence. The very notion of
preexistence causes difficulty for us because it seems foreign
and a most curious teaching. The concept, with various
nuances, runs throughout early religions of the East and Near
East. For Christians, the notion affirms the transcendence of
Christ. These early followers believed that in Jesus they had
encountered God and thus used the notion of pre-existence as
one way of saying that in the very human and crucified Jesus of
Nazareth, they experienced a reality beyond all contingencies
of space, time and history. The hymn presents the two modes
of his life: equality with God and the life of a servant. His
origin in human history includes an emptying. No mention is
made of actual origins. The expression "to be grasped" does
not in itself tell us whether Jesus already possessed equality
with God or whether this equality was to be seized as in the
case of Adam (Gen 3:5) or Lucifer (Is 14:13–14). The author of
the hymn makes the point that Jesus abandons all such claims
coming under all the conditions of the human lot, becoming a
servant unto death. To this, Paul probably added "death on a
cross." Jesus as human would be subject to all the forces that
determine human life. The cosmology of the time would recognize certain hostile forces (Gal 4:3–4; 1 Cor 2:8) that could
lead even to death. The conclusion of the hymn, however,
changes the perspective. God will exalt Jesus as the redeemer.

What other writers of the New Testament call resurrection and ascension, this early hymn merely uses exaltation. This particular passage casts light on the early theology of the divinity of Jesus rather than on his origin.

With regard to ministry, the passage exemplifies a ministry of service that will lead to death. Jesus accepts this fate willingly. God responds by raising Jesus and giving him a name above all names, the name of savior. For Paul, the Philippians are called to imitate the risen Lord who humbled himself in service unto death. They also then can look forward to exaltation. His origins are explained in relationship to his ministry and to his ultimate destiny.

The next witness to the origins of Jesus comes to us from Matthew 1:18–25.[8] Here the main character is Joseph. When Joseph gives the child the name of Jesus, he assumes legal paternity and the child is then a son of David. Matthew combines the earlier Christian proclamation that Jesus is the Son of God through the Spirit, with the tradition of an angelic annunciation of the Davidic messiah. He also adds Isaiah 7:14 to give biblical testimony to the proclamation of the angel that Jesus is God with us. In 1:25—"but knew her not until she had borne a son, and called his name Jesus"—Matthew clarifies the nature of the conception: Joseph was not the father of Jesus. Mary conceived as a virgin and remained virginal.

Matthew probably knew of an existing narrative of the annunciation of the Davidic messiah. He was also familiar with the Jewish tradition of God speaking in dreams through angels; and his community, like other Christian communities, proclaimed that Jesus is the Son of God through the Holy Spirit. He intends in the opening chapters of his gospel to go further in proclaiming that Jesus is Son of God in his conception and so joins the traditional material with the quotation from Isaiah. He concludes that the origin of Jesus is the great gift of God through the cooperation of Mary but without the usual conception through sexual union. What also appears in this episode is the comment that the conception preceded the consummation of the betrothal. Matthew begins by telling us that Joseph was troubled when he discovered that Mary was pregnant. This sets the scene for the dream sequence and offers an explanation for the pregnancy.

Matthew wrote his gospel for a mixed community of Jewish and Gentile Christians. At Jesus' origins magi are present representing those who would recognize Jesus from afar. Gentiles were welcome in the ministry of the Christian church. The ministry of Jesus will include dying as exemplified in the desire of Herod to destroy Jesus. Even those who follow Jesus can expect a similar persecution. All exist under the power of God, whether we deal with Jesus and his ministry or with the ministry of the community of Matthew. The infancy narratives express both what the ministry of Jesus will accomplish and what the Christian community will accomplish. God offers salvation to all through the Spirit of God in Jesus. God has initiated the process and God will continue the process in human history.

The final witness to the origin of Jesus is Luke. Here the principal character is Mary. The annunciation is a classical birth announcement combined with a vocation format: God calls through an angel; the one who is called questions, is assured by the angel, and a sign is given. Throughout the Old Testament the great prophets experienced something similar in their call to serve God, and significant births were announced by an angel.[9] Like Matthew, Luke incorporates the traditional annunciation of the Davidic messiah and further specifies the origin of Jesus through the overshadowing of the Holy Spirit. Twice in the opening verse of the annunciation Luke refers to Mary as a virgin. Although he does not make mention of a lack of sexual union before the birth of the child, as did Matthew in 1:25, his comparison with the origin and birth of John the Baptist in these first two chapters seems to affirm the superiority of Jesus' origins over those of the Baptist. This superiority would fail if John had been conceived and born "miraculously" when his parents were advanced in years and Jesus had been conceived through ordinary sexual union.[10]

Luke also sets the origin of Jesus in history during the reign of Herod the Great. He makes reference to Mary as the mother of Jesus and, as we have seen, probably excludes Joseph from the paternity of Jesus. Like Matthew, he knew that Christians proclaimed that Jesus was Son of God through the Spirit in his resurrection and wished also to proclaim that Jesus was Son of God in his conception. The Davidic messiah was the great gift of God to humankind by the cooperation of Mary and through the power of the Most High in the Holy Spirit.

All those associated with the origin of Jesus in Luke are faithful ones: Mary, Elizabeth, Anna, Simeon. They are also the lowly ones. Shepherds come to Jesus just as all outcasts find a welcome in his ministry. The Spirit pervades all in his origins just as the Spirit will pervade his ministry and the ministry of the church. Luke preaches a Christianity directed to all who are faithful, to all who are lowly and dependent upon God and to all who will accept the Spirit. The gospel comes to us from a largely Gentile community. The church will engage in a ministry to all in the same Spirit. God accomplishes all in the origin of Jesus as God will continue to work effectively through his Spirit in the church.[11]

For the moment let us accept the fact of an early birth. Let us also accept that the early birth of Jesus was well known. Critics of Jesus and his gospel could claim illegitimacy, but for the early believers such an explanation would be unthinkable. Jesus was the Son of God in power through the Holy Spirit by his resurrection. They also believed that Jesus was sinless (2 Cor 5:21; 1 Pet 2:22; Heb 4:15; 1 Jn 3:5), and the gospels present both Mary and Joseph as holy and righteous (Mt 1:19

and Lk 1:42). His mother was remembered as one who heard the word of God and kept it. For believers, the origin of Jesus had to be a blessed event, and if in fact Jesus was conceived before Joseph and Mary came to live together, then the conception had to be of God. At least this is a possible historical catalyst for the development of the assertion of virginal conception. The ministry of the early community involved a proclamation that Jesus was Lord and Christ. These early believers also needed to proclaim as their faith statement that God was the source of the origin of Jesus.

THEOLOGICAL REFLECTIONS

What Matthew and Luke teach most clearly is the source of Jesus: God the Father. God sends his Son into this world through the power of the Spirit. Eventually we will compare this coming of Jesus into human history with his departure. Both involved God the Father. Jesus moves into space and time through the power of God and will leave space and time as the resurrected Lord through the power of God. The motivation is also evident: love in the presence of sin. God so loved humankind that he sent his Son to bring salvation to all. Jesus was destined to sit on the throne of David and his kingdom would be forever. He would save people from their sins.

Mary cooperated with God. Jesus would be born through Mary and live a human life with a human family. He would experience all the ordinary moments of childhood and young adulthood as part of a village with relatives and friends. Though Son of the Most High, he would live a humble life as the son of Mary and the carpenter, Joseph. The divine initiative would render Jesus Son of God; the human cooperation in Mary would render Jesus "like us in all things but sin."

The New Testament clearly teaches the virginal conception of Jesus. For Matthew and Luke, his origin was miraculous, through the power of the Holy Spirit. But whether this assertion is historical or principally theological—i.e. to assert the great gift of God in Jesus—remains an unanswered question. Theologically, the virginal conception has helped to emphasize the reality of the humanity of Jesus and of his uniqueness as God's Son. It also concentrates on the divine initiative. The human race could never deserve Jesus. He was God's great gift to humankind and his miraculous conception underlies the magnitude of this gift. This belief also gives a woman a central position in Christianity. The virginal conception offers much to Christian ministry on a theological and practical plane apart from any question of historicity.[12]

The virginal conception has been part of Christian tradition from earliest days. Although "the totality of the scientifically controlled evidence leaves an unresolved problem,"[13] no one need feel compelled to deny the historicity of the virginal conception. Nor should anyone equate it with the central mystery of salvation: God is present in Jesus reconciling the world to himself. If God remains God, then a virginal conception is not the only way in which his saving presence can become a part of human history. We know that Jesus had great significance for humankind and was God's great gift. We know his mother was Mary. Like all generations before us, and like the generations to come, we shall call her blessed. Perhaps that is all we will ever know, and we should learn to be content with this knowledge.

Many readers of the New Testament willingly accept the need to place events in context. When it comes to the Christmas stories, however, many object to the search for their meaning and remain on the level of history. Certain conclusions may prove helpful.

1. Each account of the origins of Jesus, each reference by

Paul, comes from a particular Christian community with particular needs. Each reference comes from a period long after the death and resurrection of Jesus.

2. The basic meaning remains: God has given Jesus as savior to all, Jews and Gentiles. Jesus ministers to all humanly.

3. The details surrounding the origins of Jesus are not primarily historical but from the authors' experience, responding to the needs of the Christian community.

4. Each account summarizes some important aspect of Christianity. For the evangelists, the account anticipates the ministry of Jesus in the body of the gospel.

5. Each reference to the origins of Jesus finds its completion in an understanding of the church.

6. The references to the origins of Jesus respond to problems, tensions and difficulties in the various Christian communities, whether we deal with Paul and the relationships between Jesus and Gentiles or with the ministry of the church to outcasts.

7. Each reference supports the belief that God was present in the origin of Jesus and continues that presence through the Spirit of Jesus.

For the purpose of this book, the emphasis on the origin of Jesus should be on his place in human history. The power of God gave the human race Jesus of Nazareth. His entrance into our history makes it possible for humanity to see in him the human face of God. God was present in him, subject to every aspect of human life. Jesus ministered for a brief period in a tiny corner of this world. He experienced the dimensions of a human family living as the servant of all. His origin, his special relationship to God, did not preclude human development. Nor did Jesus exercise a ministry which centered on divine prerogatives. As the human face of God, he recognized God in

the faces of all others and responded to their needs. As God's
Son, Jesus made it possible for all to believe that they too are
part of the family of God as sons and daughters. The power of
God, which gave Jesus to us, supported a ministry which relied
upon an ability to see traces of God in all.

CHAPTER 3

The Resurrection

The resurrection is the central mystery of the Christian faith. If Jesus had not been raised, our faith is in vain (1 Cor 15:17). Without the resurrection Jesus was a good man, like many others before him, who attempted to bring about a conversion of hearts and failed. As risen Lord he communicates his Spirit and makes it possible for all to hope not only for a future personal resurrection but for the experience of the saving presence of God in human life. With the resurrection, Christianity becomes possible. Ministry in the name of Jesus continues.

Historical questions usually surround the study of the resurrection of Jesus.[1] What really happened? Who was there? Did Jesus really appear in Jerusalem and in Galilee? Which appearances were first? Was the tomb really empty? All such questions have some import to the Jesus tradition, but historical questions should not form the most important quest in understanding the meaning of the risen Lord. More significantly, what did the appearances of the risen Lord as recorded in the gospels mean to the original audiences of the gospels?[2] What function do these narratives perform for the church today? How does the resurrection of Jesus explain early church ministry? How does the risen Lord continue to function in ministry today?[3] Since this work deals with Jesus and the church, the main perspective will not focus on the historical questions but on the meaning of the resurrection narratives as they reflect the formation of the early church.[4]

The origin of Jesus as narrated by Matthew and Luke gives

us an opening to understand something of the community for which these gospels were written. These references also invite us to appreciate some aspects of ministry in which these communities engaged. The same will be true for the testimony of Paul to the risen Lord and for the resurrection stories as they appear in each gospel. They open a window into ministry as well as offer us an understanding of the meaning of the resurrection.

In 1 Corinthians 15:3–8 Paul offers the earliest literary reference to the resurrection of Jesus. This witness to the risen Lord has a different purpose from the appearance stories in John, the latest literary testimony. These two authors in turn differ significantly from the appearances in Luke and Matthew. Each has a particular contribution to make in understanding the origin of church and Christian ministry.

A believer often poses many questions about the meaning of the resurrection which, although never fully understood, can invite the Christian into a continually unfolding mystery.[5] The theology of the resurrection seeks to respond to the questions associated with the rising of Jesus to bolster faith and help it continue to flourish in every age, especially the scientific age in which we live. This christological perspective of the resurrection carries with it an ecclesiological perspective since Jesus and the church are inseparable.

SOME HISTORICAL FACTS

Although this study will not focus primarily on the historical, five facts emerge clearly from the testimony of the New Testament.

1. We know that Jesus was buried by the sanhedrin:

And when they had fulfilled all that was written of him, they took him down from the tree and laid him in a tomb (Acts 13:29).

2. We also know from the testimony of the gospels that the women remained in Jerusalem and the apostles went to Galilee (Mk 16:1–8; Mt 28:1–10; Lk 23:55–24:10). From this point matters become historically confused.[6]

3. We know that some followers of Jesus experienced the risen Lord (1 Cor 15:3).

4. We also know that the women of the group went to the tomb and discovered it empty. Whether the declaration of the empty tomb affirms the resurrection appearance or whether the resurrection appearances affirm the empty tomb is not clear. Each gospel narrates first the visit to the tomb before any resurrection appearances, but this might be an effort to establish some kind of chronology. The facts include the discovery of the empty tomb and the actual appearances, but which came first cannot be conclusively established.[7]

5. We know, finally, that the appearances continued for some time and should not be limited to the somewhat artificial chronology of Luke: "To them he presented himself alive . . . appearing to them for forty days" (Acts 1:3). At least we are certain that the risen Lord appeared to Paul some three years after the death and resurrection. For the moment, we will limit ourselves to these five historical facts.

EARLIEST WITNESS

The earliest witness to the resurrection occurs in 1 Corinthians 15:3–8:

> For I delivered to you as of first importance what I also received, that Christ died for our sins according to the scriptures, that he was buried, that he was raised on the third day according to the scriptures, and that he appeared to Cephas, then to the twelve. Then he appeared to five hundred brethren at one time, most of whom are still alive, though some have fallen asleep. Then he appeared to James, then to all the apostles. Last of all, as to one untimely born he appeared also to me.

Most likely the phrase "for our sins" is a later Pauline thought.[8] The idea of a redemptive death would have come later. The inclusion of "He was buried" emphasizes the reality of his death. No mention is made of the empty tomb; the reference to the resurrection follows immediately. "Raised" is typical Jewish apocalyptic language (Is 26:19; Dan 12:2). The body enters into an eschatological-type existence which is particularly evident in reading the rest of this chapter. A transition has occurred from one mode to the other (Dan 12:3), or perhaps we can say that Jesus passed out of space and time and now exists meta-historically.[9]

The reference to the third day is also eschatological. The dawn of the end-time has begun, for the cosmic eschatological process of resurrection has begun. In Talmudic texts, the general resurrection occurs three days after the end of the world (see also Hos 6:2).[10]

In listing the appearances, Paul used the Greek word *ophthe* which means a revelatory self-disclosure that is also eschatological and apocalyptic.[11] From the word alone we cannot conclude to an objective vision, since the emphasis is on the transcendent subject and not the recipient.[12] The reference to the twelve could be more political than historical following the reference to Peter.[13] This would make sense especially because of the reference to his appearing to all of the apostles after he had appeared to James. (This James is the brother of the

Lord and not the son of Zebedee.) James was the leader of the Jerusalem church, not one of the twelve, and at times his community was at odds with both Peter and Paul.[14]

The final reference to the appearance of Jesus to Paul must be seen in light of the other references to the event in Acts 9:4ff; 22:7ff; 26:14ff. "Untimely born" really could be translated as a "monstrous birth." The visionary experience with light is combined with an explanation of the event. It is not presented as open to a neutral verification or observation but as a revelatory event in which the eschatological and christological significance of Jesus was disclosed to Paul. The conversion of Paul follows this revelatory experience.[15]

The full understanding of the remarks in 1 Corinthians 15:3–8 depends on an awareness of the community to which the letter was addressed. Different factions and different values seem to divide the church at Corinth. Certain members of this community focused on the resurrection of Jesus and the event which liberated Jesus and his followers from all limits. His resurrection becomes associated with freedom, power and knowledge.[16] Such individuals would see little value in the cross of Jesus, which Paul admits is "weakness and foolishness" (1 Cor 1:18–25). These individuals who so emphasized the resurrected newness would have little interest in traditions handed on other than the Spirit. Such an approach to Jesus would create a strong individualism with a transcendence of authority, norms, laws and rules.

Paul reacts by inciting that Jesus as risen Lord has commissioned others for ministry and his resurrection does not symbolize total freedom and lack of authority. The church will function through the risen Lord, and through his Spirit the church will expect an affirmation of authority and obedience. In particular, Paul wished to maintain his own authority in dealing with problems in the church he founded.

Paul used the resurrection tradition not just for the sake of repeating the tradition but to deal with a specific problem in the Corinthian community. Tradition has a legitimate role to play in the preaching and teaching of the church. These words to the Corinthians function pastorally. "The resurrection stories were not an abstract idea for him [Paul] but a vital truth which gives value and shape to the Body of Christ."[17] They have less to say about the actual historical resurrection of Jesus and less to say about the remote future but rather express a concern for the contemporary life of the church at Corinth.

From this earliest testimony we can conclude:

1. The risen Lord was central to the proclamation of the early church.
2. The resurrection was the first instance of the general resurrection, involving a new mode of existence.
3. The empty tomb does not form part of this earliest testimony.
4. The appearances were revelatory encounters.
5. The appearances involved many people and lasted up to three years until the conversion of Paul.
6. The appearances as narrated have greater concern for the community than for the past or future.

THE GOSPEL ACCOUNTS

The various witnesses to the resurrection event in the gospels show parallels and differences both with regard to particulars concerning the empty tomb and the appearances of the risen Lord. The day of the week is the same; Mary Magdalene appears in all four accounts; the stone had been removed (by an earthquake in Matthew). The time of the visit, the number of women, the number of angels, the purpose of the visit (to anoint or visit the tomb) and the reaction of the women differ from gospel to gospel.[18]

The number of appearances also differs; Mark lists no appearances but the young man in the tomb promises an appearance in Galilee. In Matthew the risen Jesus appears to the two women who went to the tomb and then to the eleven in Galilee. Luke narrates the appearance of Jesus to the two disciples on the road to Emmaus, makes mention of an appearance to Peter, and then also narrates the appearance to the eleven in Jerusalem. Finally the gospel of John records an appearance to Mary Magdalene and to the disciples (not apostles) in Jerusalem, concluding with the appearance of Jesus by the sea of Tiberias in chapter 21.

Each gospel mentions the empty tomb, but only in the gospel of John does the empty tomb have any relationship to faith: "Then the other disciple . . . also went in and he saw and believed" (Jn 20:8). In the origin of resurrection faith, the appearances of the glorified Lord brought the disciples to believe, and this belief, in turn, interpreted the empty tomb. Even in the gospel of John the belief on the part of the other disciple upon seeing the empty tomb might well be another political reality. The episode contrasts the faith of the beloved disciple with the faith of Peter facing the same object, related more to the situation at the end of the first century than what happened at the empty tomb.[19]

In the appearances by Jesus to his followers as risen Lord, the disciples have a revelatory experience which also might be seen as church-founding and mission-fulfilling. With their Easter faith the disciples not only become believers in the risen Lord but begin their mission of preaching which also founds the church. Part of this preaching is the belief that all will rise and share in the glory of God through faith in Jesus. He returns from glory to reveal himself as the first-born of those who will be raised from the dead. In his appearances he is the same but

different. Jesus is transformed in his resurrection. He is ultimately recognized, but not at first. The resurrection and exaltation of Jesus and the sending of the Spirit constituted the
eschatological event, beginning the end time.[20]

Matthew

Matthew 28:16–20 functions as a commissioning, the establishing by Jesus of legitimate authority in the community.
The form is not unlike the common literary form in the Old
Testament as well as the New Testament in which God calls a
great patriarch, a prophet, or a leader of the community.[21] The
apostles are gathered with Jesus as risen Lord as once they were
gathered around him in his ministry (Mt 10:1–5). Thus
Matthew established a continuity between the ministry of the
earthly Jesus and the activity of the risen Lord.

The commissioned apostles must continue the ministry of
Jesus, extending it to all peoples on earth, teaching the fullness
of the message of Jesus. And his rule is for all times. Jesus has
become for Matthew the sovereign of the world, and his authority is now given to the church. Jesus called and sent his
disciples to teach and heal in his name during his ministry (Mt
10:1–4). In this final appearance he confirms his commissioning of the twelve. Although the author of Matthew presents
this as a scene involving Jesus and the twelve, in fact it concerns
issues of authority and legitimacy among the leaders of the
early churches. By the time Matthew wrote his gospel, conflicts and rivalries existed between leaders who knew the historical Jesus (Acts 1:21–22; 1 Jn 1:1–4) and others who claimed
authority based on miracles and prophecy (2 Cor 10–11).[22]

For Matthew the criteria for authority and legitimacy can

come from two directions: ascribed leadership and achieved leadership.[23] The former can come from appointment or heredity; the latter, from deeds for which the person is proclaimed a leader. Chapter 10 of Matthew presents the apostles as ascribed leaders. Chapter 28 presents the same as achieved through their experience of the risen Lord. The church of Matthew rests solidly on the apostles. Jesus has founded his church and has given the apostles the legitimate authority as leaders much as in the gospel Peter was given both ascribed and achieved leadership (Mt 16:17f, revelation by God and commissioning of Peter as rock; 14:28–29, walking on water; etc.).

The risen Lord in Matthew assures legitimate leadership for his community and mandates a way of life by observing all that he has taught. Nor is he absent from them, for he will be with them "to the close of the age."[24]

Luke

Luke presents in great detail an appearance of Jesus to disciples who had lost faith and walked away (Lk 24:13–35). Then Jesus appeared to the disciples gathered together, quite uncertain about Jesus (Lk 24:36–49). The first episode appears only in Luke. The second is a commissioning appearance similar to that of Matthew.

The first account of the disciples on the road to Emmaus has two parts: teaching and meal-sharing, not unlike Christian liturgy. Jesus first taught them the correct meaning of the scriptures. Then Jesus took the bread and blessed and gave it to them (Lk 24:31). Here he parallels the institution of the eucharist in which Jesus took bread, and when he had given thanks and gave it to them (Lk 22:19). The meal is not intended to disprove the theory that Jesus was a ghost but complements the instruction on the scriptures and thus the allusions to the sacred food of the eucharist.[25]

Throughout the New Testament, especially in Acts, the followers of Jesus are united both in doctrine and at table (Acts 2:42; 20:11). Shared teaching and table fellowship are both ministerial actions of the risen Lord. The narrative about Emmaus describes the mission of the church: teaching and the fellowship of the breaking of the bread.

The second appearance of Jesus in the gospel of Luke presents Jesus as teaching his disciples the meaning of the word, similar to that of Emmaus, and then formally commissioning them to preach. The first part of this appearance (Lk 24:36–43) serves as an apologetic function to prove that Jesus is in fact in the land of the living and not a ghost. In Luke 24:44–47 Jesus teaches. The third part of the story (Lk 24:47–49) Jesus commissions his apostles to a formal ministry which will become confirmed with the coming of the Spirit.[26]

In this second appearance of Jesus Luke presents the risen Lord as present and active in the life of the church. The same Lord who ministered in Galilee and Jerusalem ministers now in his church. He teaches the meaning of the word of God, offering forgiveness of sins. He is the Lord of all, the savior and benefactor of all, just as he is the judge of all. The risen Lord commissions other preachers to summon people to faith and fellowship with all who believe that Jesus is the Lord.

The appearance also tells us something of the church of Luke. It includes all nations. The church will call to repentance and the forgiveness of sins which implies a mission to sinners, to the lost. They still remain the flock tended by Jesus who has established firm leadership to serve and guide the community. The church is a blessed community preserving God's word and made holy by the presence of the Spirit, commissioned for bold preaching of the gospel.

The Gospel of John[27]

In the fourth gospel Jesus appears first to Mary Magdalene. The story has four distinct parts: the report by Mary to the disciples (20:1–2); the question by the angel (20:11–13); the appearance of Jesus not recognized by Mary (20:14–16); finally the recognition of Jesus by Mary (20:17–18). The movement is from panic, to weeping, to the appearance of Jesus, and finally the recognition. Mary who had initially reported bad news now is given the responsibility by Jesus to report to his disciples that he is returning whence he came. She reported first: "I have seen the Lord" (20:18). Unlike the other gospels which report about women at the tomb, in the gospel of John Mary alone goes to the tomb. Jesus both appears to her and gives her the task to proclaim his resurrection. In Matthew Jesus appears to the three women but merely reiterates the command of the angel to "tell my brethren to go to Galilee where there they will see me" (Mt 28:10). In Luke Jesus does not appear to the women.

The author of the fourth gospel was aware of the traditions associating women with the tomb, but he has changed the events in order to suit his own purpose. Since Jesus reveals to Mary that he is ascending, Mary is privileged to know the heavenly status of Jesus which indicates her special place as a receiver of divine revelation. She also is the first to experience the risen Lord, and Jesus charges her to proclaim his heavenly status. For the moment we may deduce that women held a significant role in this community since in this gospel the Samaritan woman also became a missionary announcing that Jesus was the messiah (4:26) and Martha also receives a revelation that Jesus is the "resurrection and the life" (11:25). Then Martha calls her sister which is also a missionary activity.[28]

The second scene involves Jesus and his disciples, and the third also includes the disciples but now Thomas is present.

We will treat both scenes together since they too are a commissioning scene.[29] If we combine both appearances we have
the following:

Jesus arrives and assures them with the greeting
of "Peace."

Jesus commissions them, confirmed by the Spirit.

Thomas raises an objection.

Jesus reassures them and offers a sign.

The scene concludes with the proclamation that those
who believe and have not seen the risen Lord are blessed.

Like the gospels of Matthew and Luke the fourth gospel
commissions his disciples with the emphasis on disciples. This
gospel does not give a primary role to the twelve but rather to
all the followers of Jesus who receive a commission.[30] The
disciples are to forgive sins or retain sins (Jn 20:23). Many of
the traditional features of the founding of the church are present in these scenes: the commissioning and the confirmation by
the Spirit expecting a mission of repentance and forgiveness.
The fourth gospel, however, adds another dimension. Faith
comes through hearing the word of God in the community
through the faith of others.[31] The fourth gospel indicates specific roles to the community and not necessarily to any leaders
of that community. All receive the Spirit (Jn 16:13) and they
have no need of any other teachers. Once they have heard the
word of God in the community, they continue the mission of
the community by forgiving sins and wishing all "peace."

The final chapter of the gospel of John comes from a
different hand than the one which wrote the rest of the gospel.[32] The beloved disciple, the founder and source of inspiration of the community, is dead (Jn 21:23), and the author of
this chapter has to deal with the future of the Johannine community.[33] Throughout the gospel no one shares in the pastoral
ministry of Jesus. The twelve appear basically in a negative
light,[34] and the emphasis is on the disciples, the followers, and

the role of the Spirit. In this last chapter the beloved disciple and Peter are contrasted.[35] Peter will share in the pastoral ministry of Jesus. He will feed the lambs.

The first episode (Jn 21:1–14) is reminiscent of the calling of the apostles in the synoptics. Probably the tradition of the call of Peter was familiar to the Johannine community, and the author of this chapter used that tradition to portray the role of Peter in the developing church. The threefold questioning and response is the rehabilitation of Peter after denying Jesus. The reference to his future dying will relate Peter as sharing in the ministry of Jesus to the good shepherd who will lay down his life for the sheep (Jn 10:11, 15).

The beloved disciple in this chapter still remains in a superior position; he first recognized the Lord (Jn 21:7a) and the Lord proclaims: "If it is my will that he remain until I come, what is that to you?" (Jn 21:22). By this time the beloved disciple has died and the community must make the necessary adjustment. They will accept the authority of Peter from those who trace their leadership roles to Peter, but only on condition that these same leaders recall that they are to love Jesus and give up their lives for the sheep. Finally, these leaders must also accept the testimony of the beloved disciple. They must accept his understanding of the Jesus tradition as recorded in the documents of the community.[36]

Using terminology similar to the analysis of other gospels, we can say that Peter possessed ascribed leadership, and those who claimed an authority from Peter could claim the same type of ascribed leadership. The beloved disciple typifies charismatic and achieved leadership. Peter obviously represents the traditional communities which by this time had developed a hierarchy and organization. They saw their task as handing on the Jesus tradition, faithful to what happened in the past. The beloved disciple represents the more spontaneous, charismatic community whose task was to continually adapt the Jesus tradition to new situations holding on to what is essential. The former might be called conservative, the latter, progressive or liberal.

The addition of chapter 21 by an unknown author points to the awareness that without the beloved disciple to hold the community together, the future of the church and even of the Johannine Christians lies with the organized church of Peter. The risen Lord settles the problems of the two approaches by a compromise in which Peter is accepted but the testimony of the beloved disciple must remain. Thus the church has functioned for the past two thousand years.

Some Conclusions

Just as certain conclusions on ministry can be drawn from the origins of Jesus, so similar conclusions flow from an understanding of the resurrection accounts.

1. All of the gospel accounts of the resurrection come from particular communities with particular needs.
2. The basic message of the risen Lord is cast into narrative form with the addition of vivid details and dramatic exchanges to suit the audience of the various communities.
3. Most of the details then come not from history or Jesus but from the evangelists' own way of preserving the Jesus tradition.
4. Each gospel used the appearances of Jesus to summarize the fundamental christology of the community.
5. The risen Lord and his appearances cannot be separated from the church.
6. The appearances respond to problems, tensions and difficulties in the various Christian communities.

7. Each appearance supports the belief that the risen Lord remains present to his church when they are in need.

THE MEANING OF THE RESURRECTION

In the Acts of the Apostles Peter proclaims at Pentecost that through the resurrection God has made Jesus both "Lord and Christ" (Acts 2:36). Paul in Romans proclaims that in the resurrection Jesus is designated "Son of God in power" (Rom 1:4). From what we have seen above, the resurrection is the eschatological event transforming Jesus as the first-born of many brethren. As messiah, Son of God in power, Jesus can communicate his Spirit to those who believe in him and promise them that they too shall live, for they shall rise as he has risen to eternal life.[37]

The appearances of Jesus are revelatory experiences of a transformed and risen Lord. They involve the church. What actually happened, the historicity of the events, the objectivity of the experiences, are questions which have different answers depending on the theological, philosophical or psychological presuppositions of the one responding. We need not try to solve these aspects of the mystery. Moments of faith are not usually subject to objective analysis, and these were moments of faith.

The resurrection of Jesus involves the activity of God and thus remains forever beyond complete human comprehension. Jesus, "like us in all things but sin," becomes the first-born of many brethren, the messiah and Son of God in power, giving to all who believe in him the presence of his Spirit. He continues to live in his church as risen Lord responding to the needs of his community. He lives as sovereign Lord (Matthew), the shepherd of this flock (Lk 24:13–36; Jn 21), the saving Jesus who eats with sinners and calls them to repentance (Lk 24:36–

49). Jesus is also the giver of the spirit (Jn 20:22) and the forgiver of sins (Lk 24:47; Jn 20:23). He calls his church to continue this ministry.

We still have many questions involving the resurrection of Jesus. Ultimately it becomes a matter of faith; for those who do not believe, it is all foolishness. The theologian, the believer, may have a thousand questions, and so they continue to seek understanding and still profess that Jesus is God's great gift to the human race and now he is the risen Lord ministering in his church.

CHAPTER 4

The Ministry of Jesus: Preaching the Reign of God

Jesus entered into human life through the power of God. He began his ministry by preaching the reign of God empowered by the Spirit. He preached with authority and with power. He influenced people's thought and behavior. Those who believed changed their way of living. They listened and experienced a conversion. He also influenced history. After his resurrection the same Spirit, given to his followers, developed the community of believers into a church. Since then generations upon generations experienced a similar conversion, and the world will never again be the same.

The origins of the ministry of the Christian church rest upon an understanding of the ministry of Jesus as recorded in the gospels. Granted, these documents are colored by the experience of the risen Lord, but they also express legitimate remembrances of the actual ministry of Jesus. They also carry in themselves the interpretation of this ministry as actually experienced by the earliest communities of disciples.

Understanding the source and the exercise of this ministry of Jesus prepares the reader to evaluate the ministry in the church. We begin with an examination of two words associated with the ministry of Jesus and found in the New Testament: *exousia* (in most cases to be translated as authority) and *dynamis* (translated as power). Jesus ministered because he acted with the authority and the power of God his Father. The church will minister like Jesus because it also shares in the authority and power of God.

EXOUSIA[1]

The Greek word *exousia* carries with it a certain ambiguity. In the New Testament it often can denote not just the right but the actual exercise of power. Some remarks on both Greek use as well as Hebrew and Septuagint use can further situate the word in the actual usage in the New Testament. This understanding of the concept behind the word will show how the New Testament authors saw the power of God as the basis for the ministry of Jesus. Later, this same power will form the foundation of church ministry.

Greek Use

In early Greek usage *exousia*, derived from *exestin*, denotes ability to perform an action to the extent that there are no hindrances, as distinct from *dynamis* which denotes intrinsic ability.[2] It also denotes the right to do something or the right over something, and thus carried in its meaning authority, permission or freedom. The term implies more the possibility of action, and it was used with regard to the rights of parents in relationship to children, of masters to slaves, of owners in relation to property. Of course such rights are illusory unless backed by power, and when the power was effectively present, it could be difficult to separate *exousia* and *dynamis.* The usage in classical Greek, however, roots the word in the right rather than the actual exercise.[3]

Jewish Usage

Josephus used the word as permission, as right and as authority.[4] Philo also follows this general usage.[5] In the Septuagint *exousia* first means right, authority, permission or freedom in the legal or political sense, and then was used for right or permission given by God (Tob 7:10).[6] By using *exousia* for the Aramaic root *slt* the authors of the Septuagint chose a word more aptly able to describe the unrestricted sovereignty of God than a word such as *dynamis.*

New Testament Usage

Borrowing from the understanding in the Septuagint as well as from the rabbinic word *rswt,* which at all essential points is co-extensive with *exousia, exousia* has the general sense of the right of possession of something or the authority or commission: the right or freedom to do something.[7] To be more specific: in the New Testament *exousia* signifies the absolute possibility of action which is proper to God. Two instances help in understanding this meaning:

> Fear him who, after he has killed has authority (*exousia*) to cast into gehenna (Lk 12:5b).

> It is not for you to know times, or seasons which the Father has established in his own authority (*exousia*) (Acts 1:7).

Jesus also has *exousia.* We will understand his work and his person when we recognize his authority to act. As Son of God he shares in the *exousia* of God. Jesus possesses *exousia* in agreement with the Father but also *exousia* in his own freedom in acting. Often for Jesus *exousia* implies both right and power,

for the source of both is God himself. A more detailed study of
the actual places in the New Testament where the word is used
will show how both elements, right and power, are often present, but the emphasis will be on the root of the power which is
the right, the permission, or the freedom to act.[8] Such will
form the basis for the ministry of Jesus.

Exousia *in the Synoptics*

Exousia in the synoptic gospels is best translated as authority. The word connotes a right which often implies the ability
to act according to that right, but at its root the emphasis remains on right. In his ministry Jesus exercises his right to forgive sins (Mt 9:6–8; Mk 2:5–10; Lk 2:5–10); he has a right to
cast out demons (Mk 1:27) and to teach, for his words contain
exousia (Mt 7:29; Mk 1:22; Lk 4:32, 36). The origin of this
authority, God himself (Mt 21:23; Mk 11:28; Lk 20:2), sums
up his entire ministry (Mk 10:45; Mt 20:28; Lk 22:27). We can
begin with a study of the right to forgive sins.

Right To Forgive Sins

But that you may know that the Son of Man has authority
(*exousia*) on earth to forgive sins . . . (Mt 9:6).

But that you may know that the Son of Man has authority
(*exousia*) on earth to forgive sins . . . (Mk 2:10).

But that you may know that the Son of Man has authority
(*exousia*) on earth to forgive sins . . . (Lk 5:24).

Each of the synoptics repeats the same expression. We know
according to the two source theory that Mark is the source of
this threefold repetition. Since both Matthew and Luke chose

to repeat the expression, this manifests a conviction among the Christian communities that Jesus did have a right to forgive sins. The scribes and the Pharisees objected to his claim for such authority. They maintained that such authority comes from God alone (Lk 5:21; Mk 2:7). To prove his right, Jesus cures the man (Mk 2:11; Lk 5:24b). In a Jewish tradition, since God alone can forgive sins, Jesus lays claim to share in the authority of God himself.

Authority To Cast Out Demons

Jesus also has a right to cast out demons. As a man of God, Jesus could lay claim to this right as any man of God could. Jesus also has the power to exercise this right.

> With authority (*exousia*) he commands even the unclean spirits and they obey him (Mk 1:27; see also Mk 3:15).

The distinction between authority and power becomes more evident in the Lukan version:

> With authority (*exousia*) and power (*dynamis*) he commands the unclean spirits and they come out (Lk 4:36).

As Son of God Jesus has the right and the ability to exercise this right or power. God has control over all evil spirits, whether those evil spirits can be conceived as demons or as the presence of sickness. Jesus has both the right and the power to cast out these unclean spirits.

In the synoptics authority is also given to Jesus the teacher. He teaches with authority:

> For he taught them as one who had authority (*exousia*) and not as their scribes (Mt 7:29).

And they were astonished at his teaching, for he taught them as one who had authority (*exousia*) and not as the scribes (Mk 1:22).

And they were astonished at his teaching, for his word was with authority (*exousia*) (Lk 4:32).

This verse from the gospel of Luke finds its conclusion in the reaction of the bystanders:

What [is] this word, because with authority (*exousia*) and power (*dynamis*) he commands the unclean spirits and they come out (Lk 4:36).

Luke joins authority to his teaching and his casting out of demons. He distinguishes authority and power. Not only does Jesus have the right to teach and cast out demons, but his right is exercised with power. The teaching of his word is effective just as his power to heal and to cast out demons is effective.

Origin of This Authority

Just as the early listeners of Jesus wondered as to the source of this authority, so the same could be said for followers of Jesus in any age. What gives Jesus the right to forgive sins, to cast out demons, to teach as one who has a right to teach? The answer to that question lies in the self-understanding of Jesus and in the understanding of Jesus' identity by his followers. The right to act as he did finds its root in God, as do his origins and his resurrection.

In Matthew 21 the chief priests and elders question Jesus with regard to his authority. They want to know who gave him the right to teach as he taught, to heal, to forgive sins, to act as if he were taking God's place. Jesus does not respond directly. Rather he chooses to ask his adversaries a question: "The baptism of John, was it from heaven or from men?" (Mt 21:25). His opponents refuse to answer, and Jesus does likewise. The gospels of Mark and Luke record the same incident (Mk 11:28; Lk 20:2), and although we will not find in any of these gospels a direct relationship between the authority of Jesus and that of God, no doubt can exist in the minds of the readers of these gospels. Mark begins with the baptism of Jesus in which the voice from heaven declares: "This is my beloved Son; listen to him" (Mk 9:7). Both Matthew and Luke, as we have seen, offer us stories of the origin of Jesus, and both proclaim that Jesus was conceived of the Holy Spirit and he is the Son of the Most High, destined to save God's people (Mt 1:20–21; Lk 1:35). These same evangelists record for us the transfiguration and repeat the words found in Mark: "This is my beloved Son in whom I am well pleased; listen to him" (Mt 17:5); "This is my Son, my chosen; listen to him" (Lk 9:35). If any doubt exists as to the origin of the authority of Jesus, Matthew will dissolve any questions with his conclusion to his gospel:

> All authority (*exousia*) in heaven and earth has been given to me; go therefore and make disciples of all nations, baptizing them in the name of the Father and of the Son and of the Holy Spirit, teaching them to observe all that I have commanded you, and lo, I am with you always, even to the end of time (Mt 28:18–20).

The author of Matthew not only makes it clear that Jesus has the authority of God but also, together with Mark and Luke, allows the apostles to share in this authority. Clearly at the end of the gospel the assembled followers share in the authority of Jesus to teach, to baptize and to command. But also in the body of the gospel Matthew presents the apostles sharing in the authority of Jesus. Since Mark and Luke also allow the apostles to share in the authority of Jesus, we can appreciate the different approaches of the evangelists if we compare the scene in which the apostles are given this authority.

> And he called to him his twelve disciples and gave them authority (*exousia*) over unclean spirits to cast them out and to heal every disease and every infirmity. The names of the twelve apostles are these . . . (Mt 10:1).

> And he called to him the twelve and began to send them out two by two and gave them authority (*exousia*) over the unclean spirits. He charged them to take nothing for their journey except a staff . . . (Mk 6:7).

> And he called the twelve together and gave them power (*dynamis*) and authority (*exousia*) over all demons and to cure diseases, and then sent them out to preach the kingdom of God and to heal (Lk 9:1).

In Luke 10 Jesus appointed seventy others and sent them out ahead of him (Lk 10:1). When they returned rejoicing, Jesus proclaimed:

> I saw Satan fall like lightning from heaven. Behold I have given you authority (*exousia*) to tread upon serpents and scorpions and over all the power of the enemy and nothing shall hurt you (Lk 10:19).

The apostles and the disciples share in the authority of Jesus to cast out demons and to heal. Luke goes further in including in his gospel the episode of the seventy as well as the twelve; as we have already noted, he used both words, authority and power, here as he did in the past (Lk 10:1ff). He also will include not just casting out demons but preaching as well. The ultimate ministry of the followers of Jesus shares in his authority from heaven as recorded in the conclusion of

Matthew. This church ministry finds a foreshadowing in the ministry of Jesus himself: his disciples have authority, and, in the case of Luke, the power, to cast out demons, to heal and to teach.

Fidelity to the synoptic gospels will not allow us to remain on this level of understanding of authority possessed by Jesus and shared in by his disciples. Again all three evangelists record for us a further scene that deals with the authority enjoyed by the followers of Jesus. Again, each evangelist adds his own nuance to explain the meaning of the authority both of Jesus and of his disciples:

> And Jesus called them to him and said to them: "You know that those who are supposed to rule over the Gentiles lord it over them and their great men exercise authority (*exousia*) over them. But it shall not be so among you; but whoever would be great among you must be your servant and whoever would be first among must be a slave all. For the Son of Man did not come to be served but to serve and to give his life as a ransom for many" (Mk 10:45).

> But Jesus called them to him and said: "You know that the rulers of the Gentiles lord it over them and their great men exercise authority (*exousia*) over them. It shall not be so among you; but whoever would be great among you must be your servant and whoever would be first among you must be your slave; even as the Son of Man came not to be served but to serve and to give his life as a ransom for many" (Mt 20:25–28).

> A dispute also arose among them which of them was to be regarded as the greatest. And he said to them: "Kings of the Gentiles exercise lordship over them, and those in authority (*exousiadzontes*) over them are called benefactors. But not so with you; rather let the greatest among you become as the youngest, and the leader as one who serves. For which is the greater, one who sits at table or one who

serves? Is it not the one who sits at table? But I am among
you as one who serves. You are those who have continued
with me in my trials; as my Father appointed a kingdom
for me, so do I appoint for you that you may eat and drink
at my table in my kingdom, and sit on thrones judging the
twelve tribes of Israel" (Lk 22:24–27).

In the minds of all three evangelists Jesus surely has the authority of God himself, but he chose to exercise that authority not
as one who lorded it over others but as one who willingly
became the slave of others even to the point of giving his life as
a ransom for many. The disciples share in the ministry of Jesus,
which in turn relates to God's authority, when they imitate the
master and become the servants of all. The scenario is clear:
God alone has all authority since he is the author of all, but he
has chosen to give this authority to Jesus in his ministry to
teach, to cure, to cast out demons, and to forgive sins. Jesus
then gives a share of this authority to his followers, but since
Jesus chose to exercise his authority by becoming the servant of
all, those who will share in this ministry must do likewise.

Authority in the Gospel of John

If the synoptics do not deal explicitly with the origin of
the authority of Jesus but rather emphasize the use of that
authority in his ministry of miracles and in teaching, John will
make explicit what is implicit. The authority of Jesus, the basis
of his ministry, clearly is the authority of God:

For as the Father has life in himself, so he has granted to
the Son to have life in himself and has given him authority
(*exousia*) to execute judgment because he is the Son of Man
(Jn 5:26–27).

Jesus answered them: "My teaching is not mine, but his

who sent me; if any man's will is to do his will, he shall know whether the teaching is from God or whether I am speaking on my own authority (*exousia*). He who speaks on his own authority seeks his own glory, but he who seeks the glory of him who sent him is true and in him there is no falsehood" (Jn 7:16–18).

Jesus speaks not on his own authority but on that of God. He seeks not his own glory but that of him who sent him, and thus in speaking of the authority of God Jesus fulfills his mission of being the obedient and loving Son of God even unto death. This relationship to death becomes more evident as Jesus explains:

> For this reason the Father loves me because I lay down my life that I may take it up again. No one takes it from me but I lay it down of my own accord. I have authority (*exousia*) to lay it down and I have authority (*exousia*) to take it again; this charge I received from my Father (Jn 10:17–18).

We are not dealing with just an ability to lay down his life and take it up but a right to do so. He has received from his Father an authority that is powerful. He also acts not in his own authority but only as he has received it from the Father, and this includes the authority and power to give his life for others and to take it up again. This constitutes the ministry of Jesus for the author of the fourth gospel. He will be the noble shepherd who dies for the sheep.

The relationship to life also becomes more evident in another Johannine saying:

> Father, the hour has come; glorify your Son so that the Son may glorify you since you have given him authority (*exousia*) over all flesh to give eternal life to whom you have given him (Jn 17:2).

Once again the Father who has life and has given it to the Son has given him the right to give his life to whomever he chooses. We know from the Johannine gospel that all who come to Jesus and believe in him, having been drawn to Jesus by the Father, receive eternal life and live that life with the characteristic love of the brethren.

One final use of the word *exousia* in John completes our understanding of the meaning in this last gospel. In the prologue Jesus gives to those who receive him "the authority" (*exousia*) to become children of God (Jn 1:12). In the usage in this last gospel, the word *exousia* includes not just the right but the actual exercise of that right. To understand the full meaning, however, we must root the power of Jesus in his authority which is that of God himself. He has the right to judge, to teach, to give life and to make individuals who respond to him children of God. If God is the ultimate authority, Jesus shares in this authority in his ministry. Like the synoptics, however, this authority is not used to lord it over people but ultimately to lay down his life for his sheep.

The basic theology in all four gospels is the same: Jesus exercised his ministry by sharing in the authority of God, and he used this authority for the sake of others, even to the point of death. We should recall, however, in this gospel that the twelve do not share in this authority. Jesus does not send out the twelve nor the seventy as we have seen in the other gospels. The twelve, as we have seen, are mentioned only in two episodes. The only one who seems to share in the authority of Jesus is the Paraclete (Jn 14:25–26; 16:13–15), and in the epilogue (chapter 21) Peter is given a share in the pastoral ministry of Jesus.[9] We shall return to this unusual understanding of the continuance of the authority of Jesus in the Johannine community in a later chapter.

Jesus shares in the authority of God in his ministry. His teaching, his forgiving of sins, his casting out of demons and his healing ministry are rights that he has because of his relationship to God. If God is the one who is the supreme author of all, the one who wields supreme authority, God has chosen to share this authority with Jesus of Nazareth, and this forms the basis of his ministry. In the exercise of this ministry, however, Jesus carefully distinguishes his method from that of others with human authority. He came not to lord it over but to serve. If others are invited to share in the ministry of Jesus in teaching and in healing, they too must imitate their master in the mode of exercising that ministry. As the messiah came not to be served but to serve, so his followers in leadership positions must do likewise.

Power (Dynamis)[10]

All Greek words deriving from the stem *duna* have the same basic meaning: "being able, capacity in virtue of an ability."[11] Of all the words that are derived from this root, *dynamis* is the most important. While the meaning of capacity remains, its use in classical Greek implies "power" and can be applied over the whole range of life from physical power to moral or spiritual power and intellectual power.[12]

In the Septuagint, the Greek translation of the Old Testament, *dynamis* translates the Hebrew word *hyl* which has the same basic meaning: ability, power, competence.[13] In thirteen instances, by far the minority, the word *dynamis* translates the Hebrew word *gbrh* which means strength in a sense of superior force.[14]

In the Greek world the gods have power, and certain individuals are able to exercise some control over the powers of the gods which are understood as emanations from the one supreme power. Magicians or theurgists in Greek mythology can mediate the cosmic divine or demonic forces and their interconnections, for the good or ill of others. To this context belong incantations and prayers for endowment with power. Thus healing miracles of magicians in Greek thought are acts of power. Similarly the acts of punishment in which the gods display their might are also acts of power. Individuals live in a world affected by cosmic forces which rule and affect them. Since these forces are hidden from humankind, and yet influence every individual, the person must somehow participate in them. How can a person attain the capacity and the power to rise above mortality, or, in Hellenistic terms, to be redeemed from the bondage of matter? Behind the whole Greek concept of power stands the idea of a natural force which controls, moves and determines the cosmos and which has its origin in widespread primitive notions of Mana and Orenda. These ideas will differ from the New Testament concept of power, but will have some affinity, especially when we deal with the power demonstrated in miracles.[15]

Power in the Old Testament

In place of a neutral god or gods of the Greeks, the Old Testament offers a personal God. Instead of neutral forces in nature, we have the power and might of this personal God. Certainly the Old Testament contained traces of the natural and neutral idea of power. The cursing and blessing found in Old Testament rites seems to have a manistic character, but what will distinguish Old Testament religion from the more natural religion of Israel's neighbors is the concept of a God of history. What becomes more significant is not the force or power but the will that exercises this force or power. By the power of God the people are saved in Egypt; they cross the Red Sea; they conquer their enemies. The people resort to the power of their God in all of their afflictions. Thus Yahweh is the Lord of hosts, the Lord of powers. We should also note that the power of the God of Israel is not caprice. God's power expresses his will which is determined by the content of that will, righteousness (Is 5:16). In Israel the natural basis of power in the universe is completely overcome. The power of Yahweh is completely different from Mana or Orenda. Where religion is totally impersonal, we end up with magic, ritual action and incantation ceremony. When power becomes personalized in a religious context, then we have prayer, sacrifice and obedience.

Power in the New Testament: Jesus Christ

Power in the New Testament finds its precision in the understanding of Jesus. Who he was, his origins, and how he functioned are associated with power, as is his resurrection. These we have already seen. In the conclusion of the gospel of Luke the two disciples on the road to Emmaus remark to the friendly stranger that Jesus was "a man, a prophet powerful (*dynatos*) in word and deed" (Lk 24:19). This verdict by Luke, after recounting the resurrection, rests on historical recollections of Jesus. He was a prophet endowed with power. His very existence was determined by the power (*dynamis*) of God. Luke uses the same idea to explain his origin: "The power (*dynamis*) of the most high will overshadow you" (Lk 1:35b). Luke surely saw Christ in terms of a prophetic view of power, but also perceives that at the origin of his existence a special and unique act of divine power gave him the title Son of God. Jesus in Luke's gospel bears power: "And Jesus returned in the power (*dynamei*) of the Spirit into Galilee" (Lk 4:14). With power he commands the unclean spirits and they come out (Lk 4:36). In his power (*dynamis*) he exercises his authority (*exousia*). Endowment with the Spirit gives him *exousia,* a definite personal authority which he has in substantial terms, the power (*dyna-*

mis) to exercise[16] his power in ministry. Luke presents the power of Jesus as substance: "The power of the Lord was with him to heal" (Lk 5:17). The power of Jesus brings salvation. Jesus himself is the divine miracle not merely in his origin and in his resurrection but in his actual living.

Alongside this special usage, Luke also has the general synoptic usage which describes the miracles of Jesus as *dynamis.* We should also note that his miracles are unique, for he could not perform miracles in his home town because of the lack of faith (Mk 6:2, 5).

Certainly Jesus was not the only one in his day to work miracles,[17] but his miracles differ considerably from the work of magicians whether Jewish or Hellenistic. His miracles have no connection with magic: they are invoked by the powerful word of Jesus. As Son of God, Jesus exercises the dominion of God overcoming and expelling the sway of demons and Satan. The miracles, moreover, presuppose faith on the part of both the one who performs them and the recipient. The New Testament offers no place for magic in the miracles of Jesus. All things are possible (*dynata*) only to one who believes (Mk 9:23 and par). These powerful deeds evoke amazement and praise to God (Lk 19:37) on the part of those who witness them. God is powerfully present in the Lord to save his people.

Power in John

In the gospel of John *dynamis* does not occur, neither in singular nor in plural form. We have already seen how *exousia* is present in this gospel, and it is by the combination of *exousia* with signs (*semeia*), the Johannine word for miracles, that we can understand power in this gospel. While the noun is not present in this gospel, the verb is used: "For no one can (*dunatai*) do these things unless God is with him" (Jn 3:2). His

WORD OF THE WEEK

The Subject: God ordains certain men to hell on purpose

Isaiah 64:8 - O Lord, thou art our Father; we are the clay; and thou our potter; and we all are the work of thy hand.

work - Hebrew: Maaseh-an action (good or bad); product; transaction; business

Romans 9:20-23 - Who art thou that repliest against God? Shall the thing formed say to him that formed it, why hast thou made me thus? Hath not the potter power over the clay of the same lump, to make one vessel unto honour and another unto dishonour -- What if God willing to show his wrath, and to make his power known, endured with much long suffering the vessels of wrath fitted to destruction: And that he might make known the riches of his glory on the vessels of mercy, which he hath afore prepared unto glory.

fitted - Greek: katartizo - to complete thoroughly; fit; frame; arrange; prepare. Thayer says this word speaks of men whose souls God has so constituted that they cannot escape destruction; their mind is fixed that they frame themselves.

Men get angry to think that we serve a God that can do as it pleases him. They actually think that an almighty God thinks the way they think and that he could not possibly form-fit a vessel to hell merely to show his wrath and power. Paul said he does. Men have difficulty perceiving a God that predestinates men (Rom. 8:29) on whom he desires to show his grace (unmerited favor) and mercy, that he may shower them throughout eternity with the riches of his glory. We like to believe that we must give him permission; if he is to operate in our hearts and minds. The Lord said, "My thoughts are not your thoughts, neither are your ways my ways. As the heavens are higher than the earth, so are my ways higher than your ways and my thoughts than your thoughts (Isaiah 55:8,9)". Our God is in the heavens: he hath done whatsoever he hath pleased (Psalms 115:3). He doeth whatsoever pleaseth him (Eccl 8:3). Thou, O Lord hast done as it pleased thee (Jonah 1:14). Whatsoever the Lord pleased, that did he in heaven, and earth, and in the seas, and in all deep places (Psalms 135:6). He does all his pleasure (Isa. 46:10; Isa. 44:24-28; Eph. 1:5,9; Philippians 2:13). It is Jesus that holds the keys to death and hell (Rev. 1:18), not Satan. God will intentionally cast these evil vessels of wrath into hell and lock them up for eternity because it is not his pleasure to draw them to him (John 6:44). This doctrine angers men, though it is taught throughout the pages of God's Holy Book. Men do not have a Biblical view of the living God when they think he is not in control of all things including the minds and hearts of all men. God is not only love to the vessels of mercy, but he is a consuming fire (Deut 4:24) upon the vessels of wrath fitted to destruction. We do not serve a God who is Superman that can only shake mountains, implode blackholes, and explode quasars. The God of the universe can harden and soften the hearts of men at will (Rom 9:18; Ezek. 36:26). He giveth not account of any of his matters (Job 33:13).

GRACE AND TRUTH MINISTRIES

P.O. Box 1109 Hendersonville, TN 37077
Jim Brown - Bible Teacher • 824-8502

Radio Broadcast – Sat. Morn. 8am 1300 AM Dial WNQM
TV – Mon. & Sat 10pm, Wed. & Fri. 12am Channel 176;
Tues. & Thurs. 5pm Channel 3; Thurs. 11am Channel 49

Join us for fellowship at 394 West Main Street on
Sunday Mornings @ 11:00am, Sunday Evenings @ 7:00pm,
Wednesday Evenings @ 7:00pm
Or
Watch us live via U-Stream on the web at
www.graceandtruth.net

power is the power of God given in fellowship with the Father who sent him. This same verb is used in the curing of the man born blind (Jn 9:16, 33), and it is used again in the raising of Lazarus (Jn 11:37). The resultant portrait of Jesus in John accords fully with the synoptic tradition. The differences emphasize that this unique Christ event in which he manifests power, the active power of God, initiates the new aeon and supports Christ in his entire existence.

Power in the Resurrection

We have seen that the power of God possessed by Jesus becomes most clearly manifest in his resurrection. He overcomes death. In Acts Peter remarks on Pentecost: "But God raised him up, having loosed the pangs of death because it was not possible (*dynaton*) for him to be held by it" (Acts 2:24). Death could exercise no power over Jesus, for he has life through the power of God. As the power of God gave him power in his ministry, so this same power gave him life over death. Paul also recognizes this same belief when he proclaims that "Christ is the power (*dynamin*) of God" (1 Cor 1:24). Jesus has overcome the power of darkness and death. The previous chapter has dealt with the power of God in Jesus in his resurrection. Here the reader should recall that this same power was present with Jesus in his ministry.

In each gospel we see the closest connection between the power given to Christ and the power of God. In the Old Testament individuals share in this power, but Jesus is the unique bearer. He is conceived by divine power and acts by personal fellowship with God and not through some magical means; he shares in divine power seen particularly in the power to save. God alone can save, as seen in the response of Jesus to the question of his disciples: "Who then can be saved?" (Mt

19:25). Jesus responds that God alone has the power (*dynata*) to save (Mt 19:26). The disciples who looked to Jesus as their savior knew that he brought this saving power of God and they could attain it through him. This forms part of the earliest Christian preaching found in Paul's confession in Romans:

> For I am not ashamed of the gospel: it is the power (*dynamis*) of God for salvation to everyone who has faith: to the Jew first and also to the Greek (Rom 1:16).

To this we may also add:

> For the word of the cross is folly to those who are perishing, but to us who are being saved, it is the power (*dynamis*) of God (1 Cor 1:18).

The content of both verses is the same. The word cross is substituted for the gospel but both are described as the power of God. In the message of Jesus we have the power of God for salvation. The gospel delivers individuals from the power of darkness and transports them into the kingdom of God. The power of God, the gospel, is not an empty word but a powerful word which overcomes the realm of darkness and death and Satan and brings a factual deliverance to those who will believe.

The Power of the Disciples

We have already seen that Jesus in the gospels gives to his disciples a share in his authority and ministry. The same can be said of power. If the preached gospel is the power of God continuing the ministry of Jesus, then those who preach share in this same power. In Luke he sends out his disciples with *exousia* and *dynamis* (Lk 9:1). Jesus will continue his powerful presence among his disciples through his Spirit:

> Behold I send the promise of my Father upon you; but stay in the city until you are clothed with power (*dynamin*) from on high (Lk 24:49).

This power is received in Pentecost:

> But you shall receive power (*dynamin*) when the Holy Spirit has come upon you; and you shall be my witnesses in Jerusalem and in all Judea and in Samaria and to the end of the earth (Acts 1:8).

This same power which created his own existence now creates the community of believers, sent to preach and to invite others to come to faith. These disciples also perform miracles as recorded for us in the Acts of the Apostles (Acts 4:7; 6:8).

The apostle Paul fits the same pattern. He works "through the power (*dynamei*) of signs and wonders, by the power (*dynamei*) of the Holy Spirit" (Rom 15:19). In his personal union with Christ he is able to share in the power of God through Christ. He appeals to his power in preaching and in miracles to vindicate his position as an apostle (1 Cor 2:4; Rom 15:19; 2 Cor 12:12; Gal 3:5). The Spirit is the one who dispenses and mediates power for Jesus, and through his Spirit this power is communicated to his followers. Power and Spirit are essentially united. In the Spirit the Lord is present to the apostles as dispenser of power, and in this personal fellowship gained in and by the Spirit, the apostle acts like the Lord. As a preacher of Christ the apostle Paul shows forth the saving power of Christ, and through his preaching, Christ present in the Spirit establishes believers as members of a believing community. Thus Paul has become the servant of the gospel, "according to the gift of God's grace which was given to me by the working of his power (*dynameos*)" (Eph 3:7).

The Community

All apostolic labor should ultimately lead to a community of believers. "My speech and my message were not in plausible words of wisdom but in the demonstration of the Spirit and power (*dynameos*)" (1 Cor 2:4). The saving power of God founds the community and delivers the members from the power of evil and death and Satan. The community is now equipped to withstand the powers of darkness (Eph 6:9–20). The power given by Christ is meant to be used to protect and preserve, for the full manifestation of his power over evil and death is yet to be realized. The Christian has the power to resist and to transform expressed in the wish of Paul:

> May the God of hope fill you with all joy and peace in believing so that by the power (*dynamei*) of the Holy Spirit you may abound in hope (Rom 15:13).

The hope which characterizes the Roman community rests upon the operation of the power of the Spirit. The phrase of Ephesians is significant in this regard:

> For this reason I bow my knees before the Father, from whom every family in heaven and on earth is named, that according to the riches of his glory he may grant you to be strengthened with power (*dynamei*) through his Spirit in the inner man, and that Christ may dwell in your hearts through faith; that you, being rooted and grounded in love, may have strength to comprehend with all the saints what is the breadth and length and height and depth, and

to know the love of Christ which surpasses knowledge
that you may be filled with all the fullness of God (Eph
3:14–19).

The strengthening with power for which Paul prays takes
place through the Spirit of God, and through Christ, present in
the Spirit, to strengthen his followers with his power. The goal
is the inner person resulting in a lasting relationship and at-
tachment to Christ in a manner of life and conduct based on
love. Christ's power ultimately produces Christian love. The
goal of the power which has its basis in faith and which overcomes the world is love of the brethren (1 Jn 3:9; 4:7). The
ministry of Jesus finds its completion in love.

The final expression of the power of God for the Christian
is the resurrection but will be consummated in the resurrection
of the dead: "And God raised the Lord and will also raise us up
by his power (*dynameos*)" (1 Cor 6:14). In the resurrection of
the dead the final struggle against evil forces will take place and
they will be defeated. Paul and the New Testament never speak
of an immortal soul or of a deification by magic or mysteries or
of myths that reflect the hope of eternal life. They speak rather
of the sovereign act of power which intervened in the history
of Christ and which brought about his resurrection as the only
basis of the new existence of Christians and of the eternal hope
grounded in this existence in the power of the resurrection of
Jesus. Thus we can understand why Paul writes to the
Corinthians:

> But I will come to you soon if the Lord wills, and I will
> find out not the talk of these arrogant people but their
> power (*dynamin*). For the kingdom of God does not consist
> in talk but in power (*dynamei*). What do you wish? Shall I
> come to you with a rod or with love in a spirit of gentle-
> ness? (1 Cor 4:19–21).

Power and Weakness

No discussion of the ministry of Jesus and in his disciples can be complete without understanding the place of the operation of this power. In human earthly existence, with its inherent weakness, the power of God operates. The power of God gives the world Jesus in his origins, and this same power raises up Jesus when the power of evil attempts to destroy him. Thus the power of God lies concealed both in the ministry of Jesus and in his followers and can be recognized only through faith. The death of Jesus concealed the power of God in Jesus, but the resurrection through faith manifests this power. It is Paul in particular who knows the presence of power in weakness. In human limitations and weakness the power of God becomes manifest. Because weakness was the pledge of the power of God within him, Paul could even boast of his weakness (2 Cor 4:7ff; 12:9–10). In his weakness he found freedom from self and a bond to the Lord which made him rely solely on Christ. The power found realization in the accomplishment of his apostolic mission and the attainment of the glory of Christ. When he applied this insight to his apostolate, he realized that the power concealed in weakness is the power of the resurrection just as this same power was concealed in the ministry of Jesus himself. Paul then could apply this law both to individual ministers and to his established communities (1 Cor 1:26ff). Paul's personal faith, his apostolate, and all of Christian existence rests upon the power of God in weakness (2 Cor 6:7).

The power of God in Jesus explains his origins and his resurrection and his ministry. The same power flows into the followers and into the community, but no proper understanding of power and ministry in the New Testament can prescind from this progression. We must also maintain that this power in ministry finds its conclusion in the love of the brethren even to death, and often it is concealed in weakness. The power was used by Jesus to build up his community just as the same power in his Spirit was used to build up, to protect, to preserve and to increase the early Christian communities. Power is closely associated with authority, since ultimately both can be traced to God. The New Testament, however, carefully maintains the differences even if both are associated with Jesus and his ministry and his followers. We can say that both take on a particular hue that should never be lost to later Christian communities: the authority is that of serving the community, and the power is used to build up that community. Both are interrelated and both are means to an end: the establishing and the building up of the reign of God, the true ministry of Jesus and his followers.

We should also note the meaning of the Spirit in the exercise of ministry in power. We are not engaged in some magical incantation but in the powerful presence of God as experienced in Jesus of Nazareth and continued through the presence of his Spirit in the church.

The Analysis of Jesus' Authority and Power

Certainly we may claim that Jesus as the divine Son of God possessed an absolute type of authority.[18] The source was God himself, and thus Jesus had a right to influence people's thought and behavior. Since Jesus based his life on truth and possessed a source of truth that was beyond the possibility of other mortals, he could demand a response to his mission that was absolute.

In fact, however, he did not operate in this way. The only absolute aspect of his mission was the demand that people make a response. He challenged his listeners to make a decision but did not force them to make the decision he wanted. Even to his disciples he offered the possibility to go away: "Will you also go away?" (Jn 6:67).

We can also see that Jesus had the authority of someone with knowledge. The problem for many was the origin of this expertise. "Where did this man get all this? What is the wisdom given to him?" (Mk 6:2). But Jesus did not insist that people listen to him because of his learning.

He also used legal authority, since at times he insisted that people follow the law but he would not allow the law to supersede the needs of people. His basic principle upon which he interpreted the law of Moses was love of God and neighbor. If the law was helpful for people, then the law was to be followed. When the law was not helpful for people, the law was to be ignored.

The only true authority that Jesus seemed to exercise was that of a charismatic leader. His authority lay in his person. He influenced people because individuals saw in him someone to whom they could entrust their lives. When individuals were receptive to him, they found their lives changed and enriched. But Jesus did not force anyone to follow his teachings. They could always choose to remain in the darkness, but to as many as believed in him, he gave the authority to become God's children (Jn 1:12). Jesus used charismatic authority creatively and constructively in such a way that the individual freedom and dignity of the person were respected. He could have claimed an absolute authority; he could have claimed the authority of learning and could have used the law as the means of influencing people. Instead he chose to respect the freedom and dignity of others and appealed to their consciences to listen and respond. The great charismatic prophet had arisen and people responded to him.

We can also examine the use of power[19] by Jesus. Certainly he did not exploit others but he did use manipulative power. His parables are his basic means of teaching, and parables are excellent manipulative devices to force people to come to a decision. Parables subtly draw the audience into the action and insist upon a response. A parable offers a similar situation in which the listener eventually recognizes his or her own situation and then must make a decision. Parables manipulate people into a situation in which they have little choice but to decide or refuse a decision and then, by that fact, have decided.[20]

The parable of the workers in the vineyard (Mt 20:1–16) has long been considered a difficult parable to understand. The reaction of most who hear the parable is to agree with those who have worked all day and have received the same pay as those who have worked but an hour. The objection is that the master has made them all equal while, in fact, they should not be equal. We can understand how Jesus used this parable as a manipulative device when we recall the audience and then pay attention to the conclusion: "Am I not allowed to do what I choose with what belongs to me, or is your eye evil because I am good" (Mt 16:15). The audience on this occasion in the ministry of Jesus consisted of those Pharisees who objected to the practice of Jesus eating and spending time with sinners and tax collectors. He treated sinners the same way he treated those who had always been faithful to the law. Jesus draws his listeners into the parable and then, when they recognize themselves, he asks them the question: "Why do you harbor evil against your brother? You should rejoice that I treat these sinners the same as I treat those who have obeyed the law since it is to their good fortune that they have met me and have changed their lives." These Pharisees had evil in their hearts against their brothers and sisters and thus could not allow Jesus to treat them on the same level. Jesus called them to admit that their hearts were wrong.

We have the same situation in the parable of the prodigal son (Lk 15:11–32). The elder brother harbors evil against his younger brother. Instead of rejoicing that his brother had returned, he complained. The father had placed the younger brother who had squandered his father's property on the same level as the brother who had always been faithful, and the older brother rebelled. Jesus used the parable to create the same tension. "Why do you not rejoice in the good fortune of another instead of thinking only about yourself?"

We can say that Jesus used manipulative power as well when he dealt with the Samaritan woman (Jn 4:7–42). Carefully he drew the woman into his confidence and offered her the opportunity to accept him as the messiah. She accepted and became an evangelist for her fellow townspeople.

Jesus also recognized competitive power. His disciples competed with each other, and when this type of power became evident he used the opportunity to teach a lesson on discipleship. When they discussed which of them was the greatest (Mk 9:34), he told them to become like children and to be the servant of all (Mk 9:35–37). When they were angry that someone was casting out demons in his name and was not of their group, Jesus told them that one who is not against them is for them (Mt 9:38–40; Lk 9:39–50).

Jesus was the great teacher, the shepherd, like a mother hen gathering her young. Jesus nourished his followers and used nutrient power effectively, but he did not remain on this level, for he also recognized the inherent power in the other person. Jesus exercised a power of persuasion, an integrative type of power that saw how essentially the individual must hold on to his or her own power to preserve personal dignity. Jesus would never allow his followers to remain on the level of children. He would encourage them to grow as adults so that they could assume a role in life that was worthy of their personal dignity. This same Jesus who taught his followers much as a teacher deals with the young also sent them out to teach and to heal and to cast out demons. He recognized the time when they could become his heralds on their own, and could make decisions with regard to the gospel he taught. Jesus encouraged them to fulfill their own destiny joined with him. He also recognized their own personal contribution to the mission of the messiah, and thus preserved their own freedom and dignity.

If Jesus used manipulative power and competitive and nutrient power, he directed all to the moment when they could function on their own after having made their free personal decision to follow him. Jesus did not insist that his followers always remain on the level of children in his ministry. He did not deprive them of their power to make their own decisions and respected them when they did. Even Judas was given every opportunity, and eventually when he decided to disassociate himself from the master, Jesus recognized his personal power and did nothing to prevent him from using it.

When we combine our understanding of power with authority, we can recognize in Jesus a charismatic figure who used power effectively in influencing the thought and behavior of others but never without respecting their personal dignity. His greatness included his ability to include in his ministry the recognition of power in others. His mission succeeded, and his gospel has continued to expand the horizons of human life. Since Jesus was "like us in all things but sin" we can expect to find in his personality, his life and his mission those anthropological elements common to all. Authority and power belong to the human race both collectively and individually. Jesus had to exercise both in a human fashion and did so in conformity with his understanding of human dignity and his mission to offer freely to those who believe a way of life that would allow them the greatest possibility for personal growth in the sight of God. Jesus was charismatic; Jesus used his power constructively. He used various types of power but all were directed to the final integrating power that preserved the inherent dignity of being human. The ministry of Jesus, the preaching of the reign of God in human life, was accomplished with authority and power. His disciples will continue that same tradition. The resulting church will function in its ministry in conformity to the model established by Jesus and recorded for us in the writings of the New Testament.

CHAPTER 5

The Ministry of the Disciples and Apostles

The church of Jesus Christ consists of believers who share a ministry. Each member of the community functions as a priest and as a servant continuing the ministry of Jesus. They teach and preach. They heal and work to overcome evil. They forgive sins. But within this church certain ministries have been singled out historically as empowered through the Holy Spirit. In the New Testament we can discover ministries that are proper to all of the followers of the Lord and others that are more limited to specific individuals or bodies of individuals. All can be called disciples of the Lord and can share in his ministry, but only some are called apostles, and then even in a more limited fashion we can speak of the twelve.

Disciples (*mathetes*) is a generic term meaning a follower. The gospel of John prefers this term and uses it sixty-one times. Matthew uses it thirty-six times, Luke, twelve times, and Mark, nine times. The disciples are those who freely choose to follow the Lord, to be with him, and to accept a mission. We have already noted this missionary aspect of discipleship when we recalled that Jesus sent out not just the apostles but also the seventy-two disciples (Lk 10:1–6). To follow the Lord implies a ministry of preaching the gospel. Since, however, we can understand church ministry more effectively first in dealing with the leaders of the church community, we will accept the generic mission of the disciples and concentrate

67

on the mission of the apostles and the twelve, including in that discussion the ministry of Peter, Paul and the beloved disciple.

SPECIFIC MINISTRIES IN THE NEW TESTAMENT

The study of the New Testament assures us that the early community possessed distinct ministries and operations (1 Cor 12:6, 10) but unfortunately we can obtain from the New Testament only a vague picture of these ministries.[1] We cannot tell which were considered as "orders" within the church and which were functions or offices. Not even the Acts of the Apostles gives us an accurate picture of the ministry of the early church. We read of bishops (*episkopoi*), presbyters (*presbuteroi*), deacons (*diakonoi*) and prophets. Evidently the author presumed that the readers knew the meaning of the terms used, but as for us we can only attempt to formulate a more or less accurate guess as to meaning.[2] We can understand the ecclesiastical polity only in relationship to the historical development found in the writings of the fathers of the church such as Clement of Rome and Ignatius of Antioch. We can ask today whether the exercise and understanding of ministry in the church is consonant not only with the understanding and exercise of the ministry of Jesus but also with the images that we have in the early community as witnessed in the writings of the New Testament. If the mission of the church must be apostolic, priestly and ministerial, then these qualities must also be evident in the church's ministry and in particular in the exercise of authority and power. We shall begin not with apostles, since this seems to be a broader New Testament term, but with the twelve upon whom Jesus bestowed a special share in his ministry.

The Twelve

Mark tells us that Jesus made twelve that they might be with him and that he might send them out to preach the gospel and to have authority to cast out demons (Mk 3:14ff). The clause which some manuscripts add after "He made twelve"— "whom he also called apostles"—should not be regarded as original.[3] Luke has a similar scene: "He called his disciples and he chose from them twelve whom he also called apostles" (Lk 6:13).[4] Matthew has no account of the choice of the twelve. They simply appear as a distinct group in Matthew 10:1. The setting of Mark's gospel suggests a new Israel fashioned by a new Moses. A great company comes from all Palestine (Mk 3:7); unclean spirits confess the sonship of Jesus; a high mountain forms the background and Jesus chooses twelve to judge the twelve tribes of Israel (Mt 19:28; Lk 22:30). We have no reason to doubt that Jesus historically chose twelve out of the group of disciples and also that these individuals would function within the early church.[5] In fact we have passages in the New Testament in which Jesus gives to the twelve a solemn and continuing commission.

In the last supper discourse Luke combines the making of the new covenant with the institution of the eucharist and the commissioning of the apostles. In this account Luke presents apostolic ministry in a liturgical setting.[6] The apostles will have royal authority or kingly rule (Lk 22:29). The authority within the community is expressed in the judging that will take place: "As my Father has appointed a reign for me, so do I appoint for you that you may eat and drink at my table in my reign and sit on thrones judging the twelve tribes of Israel" (Lk 22:29–30). Pastoral oversight and authority is given to the apostles. We should also note the role of Peter in this pericope. He will strengthen his brethren (Lk 22:32). The passage concludes with an implied sending out that is a stronger and more strenuous campaign than in the earlier mission of the twelve. We shall see this mission fulfilled in the testimony of Luke in the activity of the apostles at Pentecost. The apostles, the twelve, will teach the gospel and bear witness to Jesus and will execute judgment as the overseers in the church community, sharing in the authority of the Lord.

Matthew's gospel also has a solemn commissioning by Jesus to the twelve as well as to Peter. We shall return to the authority of Peter later. For the present we can turn to Matthew 18:18. Matthew uses the term disciple, but the context of this chapter limits its understanding to the leaders of the local church.[7] The gospel of Matthew is often called the ecclesial gospel since it so clearly manifests a catechetical, authoritarian and even hierarchical approach.[8] In chapter 18[9] the author will situate the leadership of the local church within certain confines to make certain that these same leaders do not exceed their appointed responsibility in the church.[10] To them Jesus will give a commission with the power of the keys (keys is mentioned only with regard to Peter in Matthew 16:19, but the same idea is present in the choice of words: binding and loosing). The metaphor of keys which open and shut the gates of heaven is easily understood in a Jewish tradition. Those who interpreted the torah possessed the keys of the heavenly doors, but Jesus is the new key to the heavenly things, and to his leaders in the church he gives this power to bind and to loose.

Binding and loosing in rabbinic usage meant to prohibit or to allow something, and then to impose penalties, to excommunicate or acquit.[11] In the Christian context the meaning relates to the forgiveness of sins. To enter the kingdom one must be forgiven and must forgive. We can see this as understood by the early community when we compare the words in the fourth gospel: "Whose sins you shall forgive they are forgiven, whose sins you shall retain they are retained" (Jn

20:23). In the fourth gospel the power is given to the disciples in clear distinction from the apostles or the twelve.[12] The fourth gospel never mentions apostles and, as we have already seen, only rarely the twelve. But in the context of Matthew it would appear that the evangelist would understand a specific order of ministry within the church. Such an order would act representatively on behalf of the whole church but would derive its authority and power from Jesus as the head of the church. This is particularly clear when we read the conclusion of the gospel of Matthew:

> All authority in heaven and earth is given to me. Go therefore to make disciples of all nations, baptizing them in the name of the Father and of the Son and of the Holy Spirit, teaching them to observe all that I have commanded you; and behold, I am with you always, to the close of the age (Mt 28:17–20).

Jesus chose the symbolic number of twelve apostles as the nucleus of his new people of God. He not only appointed them to assist him in his Galilean ministry of preaching and casting out demons but he commissioned them to exercise his own ministry of ruling, feeding and serving the flock of God after his death and resurrection. The various accounts of this commissioning in the different books of the New Testament (Mt 28:18–20; Lk 24:48–49; Acts 2:1–4; Jn 20:19–23) do not record for us what historically happened but rather present for us the establishment of an apostolic ministry that has been stylized according to the theological understanding of the individual author. We have already studied this in relationship to the meaning of the resurrection of Jesus. The conclusion that we can reach is that the twelve had a share in the authority of the Lord to bear witness to him as risen, to proclaim the gospel, to teach and to baptize, knowing that he would continue to be with them in the exercise of this ordered ministry. Finally, they would execute judgment as the leaders of the new Israel (Mt 19:28; 20:20–23; Mk 10:35–40; Lk 22:30).[13] A reading of the New Testament gives ample proof that the twelve had both authority and power to share in the ministry of Jesus.

The Apostles

We usually limit apostle to the twelve or the twelve and Paul. Such was the crystallized usage by the end of the New Testament period, but the word also has a wider sense in the New Testament. *Apostolos* in Greek means a delegate or a messenger.[14] In the New Testament anyone given such a title receives a great honor, especially when we note who is not given the title. Neither Apollos (1 Cor 3:5) nor Timothy nor Titus is an apostle. The later causes great interest when we recall that in 2 Corinthians 8:16–24 Paul tries to commend Titus to the Corinthians in every way he can think of but is unable to call him an apostle. The Didache indicates that at a later period itinerant evangelists were called apostles, but no such usage appears in the New Testament. Apostle was a more generic term than just the twelve, but within the New Testament its use was limited.[15]

An apostle bore witness to the risen Lord (1 Cor 15:7) and had received a personal commission to proclaim the gospel. In Acts Peter has a right to preach because he is an apostle (Acts 4:5–21; 5:27–42). Both Peter and John are apostles, sent out to baptize in the Spirit (Acts 8:14) and Barnabas is sent as an apostle to Antioch (Acts 11:22). Both Saul and Barnabas are apostles to the Gentiles (Acts 13:1–3). Later we shall deal with Paul specifically as an apostle. For the present the term apostle was limited to a select few who had been commissioned to bear witness to the risen Lord, could teach and baptize, and according to Acts 15 could also make decisions. As a ministry, apostleship is listed first in both 1 Corinthians 12:28 and Ephesians 4:11. The early church valued such a ministry, for in fact we can conclude that the original ministry of the early church was an apostolic ministry. When Matthias is chosen to replace Judas, Luke records that the apostles prayed that the Lord might make evident the one he would choose "for this ministry and apostleship" (Acts 1:25). Apostleship is used four times in the New Testament (Acts 1:25; Rom 1:5; 1 Cor 9:2; Gal 2:8), and taken collectively these references emphasize that apostleship rests upon a divine commissioning.

Apostles are commissioned by Christ and must be recognized by the church or at least by other apostles (Gal 2:6–9). Their mission concerns stewardship and the preaching of the gospel with an ability to make decisions (Rom 1:1; 1 Cor 9:16ff; Gal 1:1, 11; 2:2). Apostolic ministry was not meant to continue throughout the history of the church, since these individuals were founding apostles.[16] No one would again take the place of the twelve or the founding apostles when they died. The apostolic ministry of the church would continue through other ministries of the church but no longer would be based upon a direct commissioning by the Lord.

An attempt to understand New Testament apostleship will leave some unanswered questions. Since in classical Greek the word *apostolos* was associated with naval or overseas expeditions and was never used commonly for a messenger or commissioned agent, its use by the early community did not arise from common usage. A word had to be adapted to suit a new institution, but why this word was chosen remains unknown to us at this period of history. The Jews in the diaspora did not use the word, and when the new faith took roots in the west it was not translated into Latin but merely Latinized into *apostolus*.[17]

Some suggest that New Testament apostolate represents a Christian development from the Jewish legal institution of the *shaliach.*[18] This word means an authorized delegate empowered to execute a legal or personal commission for the principals represented. If in fact this offers some roots for the New Testament understanding of apostle, then we can recognize in the apostles those who represent the Lord. The final commissioning by Jesus in Matthew's gospel makes clear that these close collaborators of the Lord will share in his authority and are empowered to act on his behalf, to bind and to loose. If Jesus had authority and power from his Father in his ministry, he shared this authority and power with the apostles.[19]

Peter: His Authority and Power in His Ministry

Once we have established the existence of a group of individuals with authority and power coming from the Lord, continuing his ministry, we can examine certain individual apostles to understand just how this ministry was entrusted and how it was exercised. Peter as head of the apostolic group deserves careful study.

The role of Peter in the New Testament has encouraged numerous studies.[20] No attempt to summarize these results of New Testament research is intended in this work. Rather, the focus will rest upon Peter as one who shared in the pastoral ministry of Jesus and how he exercised this ministry.

In the career of Jesus, Peter was clearly one of the earliest called to follow the Lord, but not the first. He was prominent among the twelve, as evidenced in his name being placed first in the listing of the apostles (Mk 3:15; Mt 10:2). We should note, however, that Simon Peter did not function in solitary splendor, for in the gospel stories he is frequently associated with other prominent disciples, e.g. with James and John and sometimes Andrew in the synoptic tradition, and with the beloved disciple in the Johannine tradition.

Peter made a confession of faith in the Lord (Mk 8:30; Mt 16:6; Lk 9:20; Jn 6:69) during the ministry of Jesus. We are unable to evaluate this confession of faith, since a critical analysis of Mark indicates that Jesus did not accept this confession by Peter, but the presence of the confession ultimately accepted by the church attests to the actual profession in the ministry of Jesus.

The longest version of this profession of faith is found in Matthew:

> Simon Peter replied: "You are the Christ the Son of the living God." And Jesus answered him, "Blessed are you, Simon bar Jonah, for flesh and blood did not reveal this to you but my Father who is in heaven. And I tell you that you are Peter, and upon this rock I will build my church and the powers of death will not prevail against it. I will give you the keys of the kingdom of heaven; and whatever you bind on earth shall be bound in heaven and whatever you loose on earth shall be loosed in heaven" (Mt 16:16–19).

Mark and Luke also have a profession of faith by Peter, but in these gospels the long section on Peter as head of the church is missing. Certainly, in Matthew, Peter shares in the ministry of Jesus with authority. Matthew does not settle the exact nature of this authority, since although he singles Peter out for a special blessing from God which enables him to recognize Jesus as the Son of the living God, he does not distinguish his authority, for in chapter 18, as we have seen, the other disciples also have the authority to bind and loose. Matthew also notes Peter's weakness, for in this same chapter in verse 23 Jesus rebukes Peter and calls him a stumbling block. He who would be the rock upon which the church would be built is also a stumbling block to the Lord.[21] The authority is evident in the choice of the words "keys," but whether this is qualitatively different from the authority given to the others remains moot. We also need not settle the question whether the saying is taken from a post-resurrection appearance of Jesus and projected back into the ministry of the Lord. We are concerned more with the understanding of the authority given to Peter as understood by the Matthean church than the actual historical origins of this authority. Peter appears prominently in this gospel, and for this reason Matthew was used more frequently in a Roman Catholic tradition that stressed the apostolic continuity between Peter and the bishops of Rome.[22] But it should also be noted that the context in which Peter is given his authority is his recognition of Jesus as the Son of the living God. The authority of Peter is related to his faith in Jesus.[23]

Peter in Luke's Gospel

Several passages in Luke's gospel are parallel to Mark and Matthew, but one passage during the last supper presents another image of Peter proper to Luke. Following the institution of the eucharist he describes a dispute among the apostles (Lk 22:14) as to who will be the greatest. Jesus responds with a parabolic statement concerning the obligation of the leader to serve and promises the apostles a place of honor because they have continued with him in his trials. Luke offers his prediction of the fall of Peter in a different context than Mark and Matthew, for here the apostles are faithful in the trials (Lk 22:28). Their falling away is obliquely hinted at in verses 31–32 which form the context of the prediction of the denial of Peter and his mission to strengthen his brothers:

> Simon, Simon, behold Satan demanded you to sift like wheat but I have prayed for you that your faith may not fail. And when you have turned again, strengthen your brother (Lk 22:31–22).

The meaning of brothers here has a wider understanding than the apostles, and the strengthening refers to his post-resurrection role as described in the Acts when Peter takes on his missionary role as the leading spokesman for the faith of the Jerusalem community.[24] Peter will be the most active apostle in the Acts of the Apostles, and in that work he is given a role as a leader of the community. Again we must note that the role of Peter as strengthening his brothers is connected to faith. Jesus has prayed for Peter, and thus Peter cannot lay personal claim to faith. As in Matthew, the faith of Peter is a gift from the Father in heaven. In Luke, Simon's role of strengthening involves a hortatory or missionary function, while the role that Matthew gives Peter as rock has the function of a foundation. The former implies a continual activity while the latter is a once for all function. The strengthening aspect of the role of Peter in Luke is parallel to the role given to Peter in the fourth gospel.

Peter in the Fourth Gospel

Throughout the fourth gospel, Peter and the beloved disciple are seen in contrast. If the beloved disciple was not one of the twelve but still an eye-witness and disciple of the Lord, we can understand why he would not emphasize the role of the twelve.[25] If he also maintained an authority not based on the authority of the twelve, he would be contrasted with the leader of the twelve. In the epilogue of the gospel, however, we have noted that the editor gives to Peter a share in the pastoral ministry of Jesus.

The threefold question: "Simon, son of John, do you love me?" (Jn 21:15–17) reflects Peter's threefold denial, and thus the scene is often referred to as the rehabilitation of Peter. The imagery is pastoral, implying an ecclesial role for Peter. The shepherd feeds his sheep, leads them to pasture, and protects them. If we follow the imagery in chapter 10 of this gospel, the shepherd enjoys an intimacy with the sheep: he knows them by name and they recognize his voice. Finally, following the same imagery as found in the good shepherd parable, the shepherd will lay down his life for his sheep.

The command to feed the sheep implies an authority over the sheep, but the context for this share in the ministry of Jesus is significant. Peter must love Jesus and be willing to die for the sheep. At this period of the early church certainly some individuals exercised authority over the members of the church and no doubt some traced their authority to Peter.[26] By recalling the context of this authority the author of the gospel of John specifies on what this ministry will depend: the love of the Lord and the willingness to die for the sheep.

Certainly the imagery of authority is stronger in Matthew than in John, but in John it is stronger than in Luke. We might also note the remark in 1 Peter 5:1–4 attributed to Peter speaking to his fellow presbyters:

> Tend the flock of God that is in your charge, exercising oversight (*episkopein*) not by constraint but willingly . . . not as domineering over those in your charge but being examples to the flock. And when the chief shepherd is manifested, you will obtain the unfading crown of glory (1 Pet 5:1–4).

The emphasis is also on authority here as in the gospel of John, but the obligation toward the flock is stressed. Presbyters such as Peter will have the example of the good shepherd as the model for their authority.

Paul: His Ministry

Probably no other individual is more responsible for the actual authority and structure in the early church than Paul.[27]

The twelve exercised their authority in ministry, but their influence is largely unknown to us. We can distinguish at times the Petrine churches and can always recognize the Johannine community, but the Pauline churches predominate. Even the communities behind Luke/Acts and Matthew are closely related to the Pauline understanding of church structure and ministry. If we can study the primitive structure of the Pauline churches, we are closer to an appreciation of the development that transpired from Jesus as well as the development that has occurred from the time of Paul.[28]

Paul saw himself as an apostle. His office was questioned at Corinth, and becoming defensive he proclaims that he is "a bringer of spiritual gifts" (1 Cor 1:7); "herald of the crucified" (1 Cor 1:23; 2:2); the one who plants while another brings to maturity (1 Cor 3:6); "God's fellow worker" (1 Cor 3:9); a builder of the church (1 Cor 3:10–11); servant of Christ and steward of the mysteries (1 Cor 4:1); father of the church in Christ (1 Cor 4:15); a genuine apostle who must suffer for the sake of the gospel (1 Cor 4:9–12; 2 Cor 11:23–28).

On the road to Damascus he experienced the risen Lord, and because of this experience he claimed an authority like that of the twelve. He will submit his gospel to those who were apostles before him (Gal 1:17) and will recognize their authority to judge his preaching (Gal 2:2), but on the other hand he is expressly independent and declares that he has his gospel from a divine command through revelation which no one, not even he himself, can control (Gal 1:8, 12). His intention in dealing with the other apostles was either to show that he is not inferior to them or else to remove the question of the prestige of the other apostles from the really relevant perspective of the whole mission of the church. This perspective is the truth of the gospel. We do not know whether unity with the Jerusalem apostles was a theological necessity for Paul or a pragmatic necessity. Paul wanted to build churches with specific structures. He also wanted an identity for these churches apart from a Jewish Christian church steeped in the torah. To accomplish his task with integrity, he had to maintain a basic unity with those other apostles also commissioned by the Lord. Only then could his apostolate exist in truth in conformity to the gospel of Jesus. Otherwise he has "run in vain." The Gentile mission of Antioch depended on the decision taken by the authorities in Jerusalem.[29] For Paul the essential criteria of apostleship are common to all the apostles, and they are qualities which Paul has in the same degree as any other apostle, even Peter himself. He went to Jerusalem seeking unity and presented himself as equal to the most important man in the whole church, Cephas, and with him the pillars of the church at Jerusalem. Once his personal authority as an apostle was established, as in conformity with the gospel, then he could continue his mission among the Gentiles and could in fact establish churches that would last.[30]

Paul was conscious of his authority and would not accept any subordinate role, but he and his work were still dependent upon the recognition of the church, the source and center not only of the Palestinian Jewish Christian church but of all churches. Paul does not wish his independent authority to be misinterpreted, for he is neither willing nor able to deny the fact of dependence. He was conscious of his authority to preach the gospel and declare the wonderful things God continued to do through Jesus. He would work to reconcile Jew and Gentile, and finally he would exercise such a force on the churches that he would be founder and governor.

Paul as Founder/Governor

As preacher and founder Paul exercised a profound influence on a particular group of people. Spiritually he was the means by which the Spirit of God produced an effect on the deep layers of the personalities of the converts. Intellectually, his preaching caused a revolution in thinking, resulting in a modification of ethical conduct. No longer would they live as individuals but would form a corporate life assembled to worship, to pray, to read and expound the scriptures and to become part of the larger community. His authority was based upon his experience of the risen Lord in consort with the Jerusalem church, and he exercised his ministry by creating fundamental changes in the thought and behavior of his converts. He could describe himself as father (1 Cor 4:15; 1 Thes 2:11) or mother (Gal 4:19; 1 Thes 2:7b) who has brought them to life and let "Christ be formed in them" (Gal 4:19). It becomes clear that Paul himself is the authority and the one who exercises careful ministry to all who will listen, especially the Gentiles.

Some may question our ability to understand the exercise of Paul's power since we have only his letters, but precisely in these letters we can discover the kind of power he exercised when present himself and when acting through an emissary.[31] Personally, Paul exercised a power as a father and as an imitator. In some ways this is milder than a list of rights and obligations, but in other ways it demands more. How can one repay a debt of gratitude to the person who has given you eternal life? Paul also exercised his power through his emissaries. They were to be accepted as having his authority (2 Cor 8:23), and he expected obedience (1 Cor 4:17; 2 Cor 7:15), and they should receive financial support (1 Cor 16:11). His emissaries shared in his authority to teach, to instruct and to give leadership, and as such they not only influenced the converts but could expect to receive their complete support.

Paul also exercised his power through his letters. We have only to read the admonitions, the orders, the commands; he reminds his readers that as an apostle he commands (1 Cor 7:12; Gal 5:2; Rom 12:3). As a charismatic leader Paul demonstrated by his actions that his authority rested upon that of Jesus himself, and that although he acted in consort with the other apostles, he was independent. He would preach and reconcile Jew and Gentile. He seems to have liked the image of the one who nourishes in the exercise of power and employed every means at his disposal to use his power effectively whether that involved emissaries or letters. He knew his right to govern, and he governed with a distinct quality based upon his own commitment to the gospel.

The Beloved Disciple

The identity of the beloved disciple will forever remain in shadows.[32] As we have mentioned before, in all likelihood he was not one of the twelve. Probably he became a follower of Jesus in Jerusalem and was an eyewitness to the events surrounding the death and resurrection.[33] Unless he was an eyewitness his authority would be questionable, especially since his gospel takes an unusual approach to Christianity.

The beloved disciple founded a community and was the primary authority figure. He taught his community the meaning of the Jesus tradition, emphasizing what he considered the essential characteristics of Christian faith: a personal commitment to the Lord and a profound love of the brethren.[34] His gospel manifests an approach to governance based upon this twofold approach to Jesus without the necessity of other teachers apart from the Spirit:

> The counselor, the Holy Spirit whom the Father will send in my name, will teach you all things (Jn 14:26).

> When the Spirit of truth comes he will guide you into all the truth (Jn 16:13).

Jesus alone in the first twenty chapters of the gospel has authority. He does not send out the twelve nor the seventy-two. The Spirit alone will share in the ministry and authority of Jesus over the flock,[35] and thus the type of authority manifested in this gospel could be called charismatic. The person filled with the Spirit of Jesus exercises authority. The author does not explain how we can know the presence of this Spirit. Surely the Spirit remained with the beloved disciple. Presumably the Spirit also remains present to those who have made their faith commitment to the Lord and demonstrate a love of the members of the community, even to the point of giving up their lives for a single member of that community. The new commandment is to love the way Jesus loved (Jn 13:34), which includes a willingness to die for the sheep just as the good shepherd would lay down his life for his sheep (Jn 10:15).

The authority of the beloved disciple seems to have been questioned by the early church, for in the third letter of John we read:

I have written something to the church, but Diotrephes, who likes to put himself first, does not acknowledge my authority. So if I come I will bring up what he is doing, prating against me with evil words. And not content with that, he refuses himself to welcome the brethren, and also stops those who want to welcome them and puts them out of the church (3 Jn 9–10).

No doubt the beloved disciple claimed an authority equal to that of anyone else in the early church, but the mode in which he exercised this authority in his own community seems to have been through a gentle approach to Christianity based on the essential elements. His gospel, unlike that of Matthew, does not end with a command to the twelve but with a testimony calling for faith (Jn 2:31).[36]

The final chapter of this gospel, added by an editor after the death of the beloved disciple, brings an understanding of authority and pastoral ministry in the Johannine community to a conclusion. In this chapter, as we have already seen, Peter is given a share in the ministry of Jesus to care for the sheep. Three times Jesus asks Peter: "Do you love me?" (Jn 21:15–17). Three times Peter responds affirmatively, and three times Jesus commends his sheep to Peter's care. The context of this share in the ministry of Jesus founds his ministry: a love of Jesus and a willingness to die for the sheep. For anyone to share in the pastoral ministry of Jesus, he must be willing to follow the example of the good shepherd (Jn 21:18–19). The final editor of this gospel would accept the authority of Peter and his successors but would remind those who shared in this authority of the conditions for its exercise.[37]

The beloved disciple is depicted as superior to Peter throughout this gospel: he reclines on the breast of the Lord at the last supper (Jn 13:23–26); he had stood faithfully at the foot of the cross (Jn 19:26–27); he ran to the tomb first and believed (20:8); he recognized Jesus on the shore (Jn 21:7); he never had to be rehabilitated, as did Peter, for he never denied the Lord, and was given a promise that his testimony would remain (Jn 21:22–24). The authority of the beloved disciple rests upon his testimony which is the gospel of John.

OFFICES AND MINISTRIES IN THE EARLY CHURCH

In the development of the church the early local communities came under the pastoral rule of *presbyteroi* (elders) or *episkopoi* (overseers). The words seem to be used interchangeably.[38] Possibly the origin of these offices can be traced to two different strains of Judaism influencing early Christianity. In Pharisaic Judaism the *zeqenim* (elders) set policy but were not responsible for the spiritual care of the community. In sectarian Judaism, e.g. in Qumran, the *mebaqqer pa qid* (supervisor or overseer) had a pastoral responsibility. Perhaps not all the presbyters assumed the role and title of supervisor.[39]

We are not certain of the functions of these ministers, but we do know something of their qualifications as found in 1 Timothy 3:8–11. They had responsibility for common goods because they must rule their own houses first (1 Tim 3:1–7); they taught (1 Tim 5:17), and they seem to have had a pastoral role of shepherding (Acts 20:28; 1 Pet 5:2). Together with *presbyteroi* and *episkopoi* the early church also functioned through the ministry of *diakonoi* (servers) and *neoteroi* (younger ones). Again both words were used interchangeably.[40] As an office this appears only in Philippians 1:1 and in 1 Timothy 3:8, 12. They appear to have been assistants to the overseers and were given authority to preach and baptize and were related to the seven in Acts 6–8.

These principal ministers in the early church continued the ministry of Jesus through appointment by the apostles. They taught, they baptized and they governed the communities. We have little knowledge of their actual ministry, but can detect some abuse when we read the admonition in 1 Peter to follow the example of the good shepherd:

> So I exhort the elders among you, as a fellow elder and a witness of the sufferings of Christ as well as a partaker in the glory that is to be revealed, tend the flock of God that is your charge, not by constraint but willingly as God would have you, not for shameful gain but eagerly, not as domineering over those in your charge but being examples to the flock. And when the chief shepherd is manifested you will obtain the unfading crown of glory (1 Pet 5:1–4).

The early leaders were supposed to follow the example of the good shepherd in the exercise of their ministry. The early church would not lose sight of the ideal of leadership as exercised by Jesus and would remind those who would eventually share in this ministry about the conditions upon which it rests. No doubt some had abused their authority in the exercise of their power, and the author of 1 Peter calls them to task to reexamine their ministry.

Variety of Ministries

In three places in the New Testament a list of ministries appears: 1 Corinthians 12:4–7, Ephesians 4:11, and Romans 12:6–8. 1 Corinthians speaks of: apostles, prophets, teachers, wonder-workers, healers, helpers, administrators, speakers in tongues. Ephesians lists: apostles, prophets, teachers, shepherds and evangelists. Romans speaks of three functions: prophesying, serving and teaching. Each minister contributes to the church, and each one builds up the community by his or her ministry. These three lists hardly give us a coherent picture of the ministry of the apostolic church but they were not intended to do so. Each was written in the course of a practical instruction on the duties of churchmanship as these tasks were to be performed by members of the community. We are not aware of the precise nature of the authority of these individuals but only that somehow all of these ministries had a share in that ministry and all contributed to the community. In these ministries the Lord gave a share in this authority "for the perfecting of the saints, to the work of ministering, to the building up of the body of Christ" (Eph 4:11).

The Exercise of Ministry in the Early Church

The early community continued the ministry of Jesus in the role of the twelve, the apostles, and other ministries. In every instance, however, the ministry was based on the paradigm created by Jesus. They would preach and teach; they would forgive sins; they would heal and work miracles; they would baptize and gather the community together; they would rule the church after the example of the good shepherd.

To account for the rapid expansion of Christianity we must recognize in these early leaders the charismatic authority made possible through the communication of the spirit. The example of the good shepherd offers a nutrient type of power. The presence, however, of many individuals in the church community with various contributions to make to the building up of the body of Christ points to an integrative type of power. Both existed in early Christianity.

No doubt some holders of office attempted to exercise an absolute type of authority that might at times be termed autocratic. Paul had to react to the authority of Peter or of the leaders of the Jerusalem church, but his motivation cannot be forgotten: he needed the proper authority to build Gentile churches and would not create obstacles for the inclusion of Gentiles into the Christian community.

Paul himself was charismatic. When necessary, however, he appealed to his commission as an independent apostle and established rules under which the nascent church could flourish in Gentile communities. He proposed to be a gentle father or mother but also recognized the need for his followers to assume personal responsibility and allowed many of his followers to become his co-workers in the Lord.

Peter exercised an authority as the leader of the twelve but apparently in consort with them. Since 1 Peter is attributed to him, we might presume that he followed the example of the good shepherd in how he exercised his authority, and tradition tells us that in fact he gave his life for the sheep.

The beloved disciple was also a charismatic figure who exercised control over the Johannine community, but his power lies more in his testimony of faith in the Lord and the love of the brethren. Like the good shepherd he wanted to maintain the authority and ministry of Jesus through faith and love.

For the rest of those in authority in the early church we can only say that they were admonished to follow the example of Jesus and exercise an authority in ministry by service, nourishing the community and recognizing the contribution that each member could make to the building up of the church. The authority of Jesus remained but always based upon the example of the Lord who gave his life in service for all.[41]

CHAPTER 6

From Community to Communities;
From Churches to Church

The ministry of preaching, healing, casting out demons and forgiving sins continued through the efforts of those who believed in Jesus. He had gathered his followers around him in his ministry, and now this little community once again was united through his Spirit. They had experienced the risen Lord and become bold in their proclamation of Jesus as Lord and Christ (Acts 2:36). Like Jesus, these first missionaries led the life of traveling preachers waiting in expectation of the speedy return of Jesus in glory. Originally directed to Jews, these Christian preachers quickly extended their preaching of the gospel to Gentiles. With the passing of time as the teachings of Jesus spread, institutional forms and structures became tighter. What began as a gathering of Jews who believed in Jesus became local churches of both Jews and Gentiles. Before the end of the first century this new movement became a church heavily dominated by Gentiles.

In recent years many scholars have attempted to fill out this development.[1] Unfortunately they all face the lack of "hard facts." We have only possible interpretations. One fact seems clear: the church as we know it developed slowly. This in turn gives rise to a theory.[2] Christianity presupposes a fundamental solidarity and equality among believers without master-servant relationships. Such a theory need not exclude authority and leadership and the actual exercise of that authority, but the basis remains forever solid. The baptismal declaration, "There is neither Jew nor Greek, freeman nor slave, for you are all one in Christ Jesus" (Gal 3:28), remains forever the foundation of the Christian community.

The development from the death and resurrection of Jesus to the organization of Ignatius of Antioch and Clement of Rome lies forever in shadows. We do not have complete historical records; we do not have clear sociological analysis. We have only the writings of the New Testament and our knowledge of Greco-Roman organizations and Jewish institutions. From the former we can detect some possible avenue of development. From the latter we can compare practices in the early Christian community with their social and cultural context.

COMMUNITIES OF CHRISTIAN BELIEVERS

In the common Greek of this period, *ecclesia* (church) denoted the assembly of the free male citizens of a city.[3] In Hebrew the assembly of the Lord was called *qehal*. When the Old Testament was translated into Greek, *qehal* was sometimes translated as *ecclesia* and other times as *synagoge*. The Christians began to refer to themselves as the *ecclesia* of the Lord. The term was used for the free association of Christians assembled at the house of a member, for the various house communities of a city (e.g. the church which is in Corinth), for Christian communities in several cities, and finally for all Christians in the world.[4] The word *ecclesia* can refer to the actual assembly of Christians or the Christian group itself whether local or dispersed as many house communities all over the world. For Christians of the twentieth century, to use the word "church" usually refers to the worldwide organization. Such a usage would be anachronistic when referring to the New Testament.

The early Christians made the *oikas* (house) the pastoral basis for the Christian movement: the *ecclesia* of the house of

Aquila and Priscilla (1 Cor 16:19), of Prisca and Aquila in Rome (Rom 16:5), the house of Nympha (Col 4:15). The earliest structure in Christianity followed the general unit of civic life: the household. Such a household contained members of the family as well as servants and slaves. Early Christian groups built their proper structure on already existing relationships, both internally (members of the household) and externally (friends, acquaintances, etc).[5] Different households existed within different cities, which also gave rise to the various approaches to the Jesus tradition which we call the gospels. Some of these communities have left us their understanding of the Jesus tradition in the gospels we call Matthew, Mark, Luke and John.

The house in these early Christian communities provided the forum for preaching and instruction; they gathered there, ate and drank, and celebrated the eucharist (Acts 2:40–47). Sociologically, the heads of these households were wealthy citizens who placed their houses at the disposal of the communities. The communities themselves, however, consisted of various levels of society. Such a structure continued down to the third century. In the early fourth century Christians could have separate church buildings, but until then the basic unit of society formed the structure into which the early Christian community fit.

In Roman and Hellenistic society the father of the house exercised the authority for all. The structure in ancient times was clearly hierarchical with a patriarchal order. Initially the Christian community broke up this hierarchical and patriarchal structure, since the community consisted of brothers and sisters, united in one faith, one Lord and one baptism. Eventually the hierarchial and patriarchal model predominated, as we shall see in the development of church structure by the end of the first century.

As with any society, eventually these house communities

faced the question of structure and authority. Who is in charge? How are conflicts resolved? Who establishes relationships with other house churches? Who sets the rules and how must they be followed? If any people think that the early Christian community existed without conflict, they have only to read carefully the Acts of the Apostles, the letters of Paul, and finally the other writings of the New Testament. Conflict may not have predominated, but conflict flourished even among the leaders of the Christian community.

The first fundamental conflict arose in Antioch at the beginning of the missionary work of Barnabas and Paul. Christianity struggled with the split between those who saw the teachings of Jesus as a system of doctrine and a code of ethics and those who saw the teachings of Jesus as a proclamation of the redemptive act of God in Jesus by which God opened the way through faith to reconciliation. The former position is that of James and the community at Jerusalem. The later position is Paul's. The earliest conflict involves Jewish Christian relationships as well as Jewish Christian and Gentile Christian relationships. During the initial period of the Gentile mission, no effort was made to coordinate that mission with the type of Christianity associated with Jerusalem. The Jerusalem community saw the Jesus tradition as an outgrowth of Judaism with its observance of the law. Soon, however, the law-free gospel of the Gentile church came into conflict with the legal framework of Jewish Christianity. The dispute came to a head at Antioch with the conflict portrayed in Galatians 2:11–13.

The council of Jerusalem convened, and it determined that Gentile Christians were free from circumcision but were obligated to observe those laws required by Leviticus of non-Hebrews living in the midst of Hebrews. Harmony was restored, and Paul was free to continue his missionary activity in good conscience free from any harassment by those who wanted all Christians to first become Jews. All of this is recorded in Acts 15. Paul continued his successful activity as missionary and, but for his arrest in Jerusalem, he would have continued his preaching in the west. Acts may have erred chronologically but has recorded the successful resolution of the conflict between Paul and the leaders of the Jerusalem church. Almost from the beginning early Christian ministry involved questions of leadership, authority and power.

In the resolution of this conflict we have the beginning of some established authority to resolve conflicts: church leaders assembled together have some authority over households of Christians existing in different and distant cities. The church at Jerusalem has authority, since James, the brother of the Lord, is accepted as continuing the accurate interpretation of the Jesus tradition.

Such is the traditional understanding of the resolution of this conflict. Another interpretation is also possible.[6] The apostolic decree of Acts 15 is understood not as the result of the conflict in Antioch as recorded in Galatians 2:11–14 but as the cause. If we follow the hint given in Luke that the dispute between Paul and Barnabas that resulted in their separation (Acts 15:36–40) was subsequent to the Jerusalem conference, then we can take seriously the opinion that the dispute at Antioch was the result of this conference. Thus there is no future conference to which we can speak to restore the unity that was fractured in Antioch. The scenario might be the following:

1. Paul goes to Jerusalem with James, Peter and John (Gal 2:6b–10); the result is that Gentiles have freedom and Paul is reminded to remember the poor. No other obligations are involved.
2. The apostolic decree is formulated (Acts 15); Paul was not present.
3. Paul learns of the apostolic decree and confronts Peter, Barnabas, and the men from James in Antioch.

4. Paul loses. Peter and Barnabas and others withdraw
from table fellowship with those Christians who do
not observe the Jewish law.

Up to this point Paul felt secure he was preaching a gospel
with the support of the Jerusalem church and with the support
of the Antioch community. After the dispute, Paul lost his
power base in Antioch, and as Acts confirms, he had to travel
farther west hoping to find acceptance for his missionary
preaching. He wrote to the Romans, modifying his views but
still maintaining his fundamental gospel of freedom. The tension between Jewish and Gentile Christianity which had been
present from the beginning of the Christian mission as reported in Acts was never resolved. Thus Paul never preached to
the Gentiles without the harassment from those who disputed
his understanding of the Jesus tradition. He may have ended
his career as an isolated figure whose theological insights and
emphases were destined for decline in subsequent centuries.

Obviously the defeat of Paul at Antioch did not mean that
Paul was eliminated from the memory of the church. We have
already seen him as a hero in Acts, and his letters have come
down to us. He was remembered as an apostle, a missionary and
a martyr for the faith. But the latter remains more common in
the tradition than his teachings. The dispute at Antioch meant
that the interpretation of the faith other than that of Paul became normative for Christian ministry. Luke in particular por-
trays this in Acts.

In the Acts of the Apostles Luke replaces the Paul of Galatians, and also in a limited fashion in Romans, with the Paul
who will compromise his view for the sake of the unity of the
church and the church authorities. Luke presents Paul as the
theologian who gives full support to the apostolic decree as
well as the one who dutifully returned to Jerusalem to submit
himself to church authorities (Acts 21:20–26). This will fit in

well with the images we have of the church in the pastorals as we shall see shortly. Christianity was quickly becoming an organized church with a system of doctrine and code of ethics. Such was the outgrowth of the original preaching that acknowledges God's redemptive acts in Jesus and still present in a gathering of disciples.

The recollection of this unresolved dispute did not disappear with the composition of the canonical New Testament. Marcion, for example, seems to have justified his preference for Paul by referring to Paul's condemnation of Peter. For Marcion, Paul had the true Christianity rather than Peter. The Valentinians also shared this view, accepting Paul as the superior apostle. Ultimately what happened was that those who favored Peter were thought to be those who were right, "orthodox." Further evidence might be found in Matthew 16:17–18 wherein Peter is exalted as the "rock of the church." Perhaps this combated the self-exaltation of Paul and his authority in Galatians 2:11–13. The apostolic decree with its emphasis on doctrine and ethics was followed long after salvation by grace through faith ceased to be regarded as the touchstone of the Christian faith.

Paul lost in his effort to influence the theological understanding of Christian ministry in the early church. The community preserved his letters but often interpreted them in a way different from his intention. The later church even added to his authority the pastoral epistles which clearly differ from the teachings of the early Paul. Although he may have lost the battle, Paul's teachings in Galatians and Romans continue to challenge the church to recall the fundamental aspect of the Jesus tradition which emphasizes justification through faith alone.

For the first thirty years after the death of Jesus the early communities struggled with authority, with the resolutions of conflicts, with organization, with theology, and with the true meaning of Christianity. They also faced the thorny question of relationship to Judaism and found themselves embroiled in a future which seemed to imply a long delay of the parousia and the influx of Gentiles. In many ways these conflicts remain unresolved. Even the development of the "church" in the final third of the first century could not answer all of these profound questions. Certain decisions were made from which we have developed the church we now know as the Christian church. Things might have been different but they are not. The system of doctrine with orthodox teachers and the code of ethics with careful observation became the hallmarks of Christianity.

The Church of Matthew

The gospel of Matthew alone among the gospels, as already noted, uses the word *ecclesia* (church). Often scholars call it the ecclesial gospel, and through the centuries the church used this gospel for liturgy and for catechetical purposes. The Roman Catholic Church in particular has particularly favored this gospel. Not until the reforms of the liturgy of the Second Vatican Council have Roman Catholics listened to the other gospels in their liturgy on a regular basis. All Christians, and many non-Christians, have heard of the sermon on the mount. Few realize that Luke has a similar sermon on the road to Jerusalem. Everyone knows that Christianity has eight beatitudes (Matthew); they often do not know that Luke lists four. No doubt Matthew has influenced centuries of Christian history.

For our purposes here we are concerned with the community of Matthew which probably flourished in the 70s in Antioch.[7] The community was a mixed community of Jewish and Gentile Christians. The author, probably a scribe, perhaps referred to himself in saying: "Every scribe who has become a disciple of the reign of God is like a householder who brings out of his treasure what is new and what is old" (Mt 13:52). This follower of the Lord realized that the future of Christianity belonged to the Gentiles. He also accepted the delay of the second coming and prepared for future generations by offering guidelines for an established, organized and even hierarchical church.[8] Once Paul lost out in Antioch he retreated to Asia Minor where he could preach his gospel more freely. The gospel of Matthew represents a compromise conciliating the more stringent position of James and the more liberating opinion of Paul.[9] The author of Matthew admitted that the law continues to bind but must be radically interpreted by the Jesus tradition. This compromise by Matthew continues throughout the centuries, and the church flourishes when the efforts at compromise and conciliation permeate its structure.

Matthew expects Jewish and Gentile Christians to live in peace. He begins his gospel with magi coming from the east to worship the new-born king of the Jews (Mt 2:1–5). He ends his gospel with the command "to make disciples of all nations" (Mt 28:19). Through the gospel the author makes reference to Jewish traditions while being open to Gentile development. This wise Jewish Christian seems to have seen both sides of an issue and patiently sought resolution by compromise and conciliation.

The ecclesial gospel becomes the pastoral gospel.[10] Luke comes down hard on the rich. Such is not the style of Matthew. The rich may find it harder to enter the kingdom of God (19:23) but they can always be poor *in spirit*. If not physically hungry they can hunger after justice (Mt 5:3, 6). Even the weeds that grow in the church should not be torn out but tolerated with patience and mercy (Mt 13:24–30). The story of the coin in the mouth of the fish (Mt 17:24–27) also exemplifies this tendency to compromise. Although the followers of Jesus are not obliged to pay such taxes, this exercise of Christian freedom should be avoided if it might cause offense. This also seems to have been the principle at issue in the dispute between Peter and Paul and Antioch. Paul proclaimed that Christians need not observe the dietary laws of the Jews. Peter evidently went along but backed away when this caused problems. Peter chose to compromise rather than destroy unity. Even in church authority Matthew seeks a middle position. He recognized the need for authority and leadership but chose Peter who was acceptable to both Jewish and Gentile Christians as his model for both authority and leadership. He confers upon Peter the power to bind and loose in chapter 16. In chapter 18, however, a chapter directed in particular to church leaders, he also confers this power to the church.

The community of Matthew represents a community with great respect for law and for authority. He also seeks conciliation and compromise wherever possible. In the past many readers of Matthew (including this author) looked upon this gospel as rigid. If the emphasis remained only on law and authority, the gospel would be rigid. The presence of the conciliating spirit changes an authoritarian gospel to one which recognizes the need for nuances and compromise. For those who fail to see this second aspect of the Matthean community, the temptation to legalism and authoritarianism abounds. Matthew allows no such conclusion. Perhaps this is no better manifested than in his ideas in chapter 18.

Many scholars call this chapter, as already noted, the ecclesial chapter of Matthew.[11] It begins with the question of who is greatest in the reign of God or greatest in the church. Jesus responds by offering the example of a child. The one who is dependent upon God and on others is greatest. The church leader, the church member, anyone who recognizes the need for relying upon God and upon the members of the community, is the greatest in the church.

The next section (Mt 18:5–9) deals with scandal in the

church. All, especially leaders, take care about harming those who are most vulnerable in the community. Scandals given by those promised as church leaders can hurt the most. Sometimes those who are weakest can be hurt the most and be lost to the community forever.

The chapter continues with an injunction to seek out the lost sheep. Both church leaders and members must always seek out the one who has strayed and welcome that person back. The church that cares little for the one member who has wandered off no longer continues the tradition of Jesus.

In dealing with discipline in the church Matthew offers guidelines. When problems arise, go first to the party involved. First seek reconciliation personally. Then call in a few others, and afterward the church will decide. Finally the person is to be treated "like a Gentile and tax collector" (Mt 18:17). Some have interpreted this as an expulsion with the shunning of the former church member. Brown differs in his interpretation. "Is the officially repudiated Christian now to be shunned totally, or is he to be the subject of outreach and concern in imitation of Jesus who was so interested in searching out tax collectors that he was accused of being their friend (11:19)?"[12]

The final section involves forgiveness (Mt 18:21–35). Christians, both leaders and members of the church, forgive without limit. The power to forgive must characterize Christianity more than the power to excommunicate. People will not turn from Christianity if it is too forgiving. People have turned from Christianity in droves because they found it unforgiving. The unforgivable sin is to be unforgiving.

The church of Matthew needed organization to survive in a sinful world. Someone had to be in charge; rules had to be made and observed; structures had to be established. The presence of all such elements in Christianity must never, however, take away from the call of Jesus to the lost with an infinite abundance of forgiveness. The church of Matthew never settled for black or white. Gray often permeates in life, and when things go askew, we always have the example of Jesus who calls for forgiveness seventy times seven.

The Community of Luke

Chronologically the next Christian community exemplified in the New Testament gospel tradition comes from the study of the gospel of Luke and the Acts of the Apostles. From the opening prologue, the author centers on continuity. The believing community in the 80s must feel comfortable that what they accept as the meaning of the Jesus tradition in fact can be traced back through ministers of the word to eyewitnesses to Jesus (Lk 1:1–4). The same continuity persists in the development of the Acts. The gospel ends in Jerusalem. Acts begins in Jerusalem and concludes when Paul preaches the gospel of Jesus in Rome, "openly and unhindered" (Acts 28:31).

The sense of tradition roots this continuity but the Spirit makes it all possible. Throughout the gospel and Acts, the Spirit figures prominently. The gospel begins with the Spirit coming upon Mary (Lk 1:35). The same Spirit inaugurates the church at Pentecost (Acts 2:1–5). Seventy times Luke uses the word *pneuma* (Spirit) in Acts. Peter and Paul in Acts are remembered not primarily for their personal exploits, but as vehicles of the Spirit. The disciples must not look longingly for Jesus in the heavens (Acts 1:11) but recognize the power of the Spirit on earth. This Spirit will accomplish the spread of the Jesus tradition to the center of the known world. With the experience of Pentecost, the apostles become bold in their proclamation. Subsequently, all those who will become followers of the Lord will be endowed with the Spirit from on high (Acts 2:38; 8:15–17, etc.). This same Spirit directed Peter to the house of Cornelius, gave the impetus for the missionary activity of Barnabas and Paul, and is proclaimed as the inspiration for the apostolic decree in Acts 15. Paul goes to Rome through the guidance of the Spirit (Acts 19:21), and when leaving Asia for Europe the Spirit provides presbyters for the flock (Acts 20:28). Every step in the development of Christianity from a small group in Israel to a worldwide church results from the activity of the Spirit.

The community of Luke takes pride in its origin and its accomplishments. The community moves from triumph to triumph until the gospel reaches Rome. All is made possible through the power of the Spirit which continues to live in the Christian community. Christians may walk tall, secure in their foundations and confident in the future. Setbacks are temporary, for no one can thwart the positive and forward movement of the Spirit.

Such a viewpoint of the Christian church, however, has its drawbacks. Triumphalism recurs frequently in the annals of the church. Such an attitude differs significantly from the power in weakness which lies at the root of the Jesus tradition. Christianity does not go from triumph to triumph in spite of all efforts to whitewash failures. A community of the Spirit makes eminent sense provided that community does not lay claim to controlling the Spirit or limiting the Spirit. If only church leaders have the Spirit, if only church leaders can interpret the Spirit, then failures are inevitable. The Spirit surprises and even allows one generation of Christians to pay for the foolishness of an earlier generation. A church of the Spirit in which all have the Spirit also offers problems. If all share in the same Spirit, then the church needs no authority or leadership. This approach to the church has led to anarchy.

Luke has his approach to the future church. A sense of pride and accomplishment is good. An awareness of the powerful presence of the Spirit invigorates. One approach, however, is not enough, for the Jesus tradition shines more brilliantly than any facet can reflect. Luke makes his contribution to ecclesiology and allows others to make theirs.

The Community of John

I have already made frequent references to the Johannine tradition. We need not retell the contributions made by the beloved disciple and his community. Certain elements should, however, be highlighted. This community offers a unique approach to the church which should remain just as the testimony of the beloved disciple will remain (Jn 21:23). Historically the witness of the fourth gospel has frequently proven troublesome to the organized church. For that reason alone it merits careful understanding.

The community of the beloved disciple emphasized the individual relationship to Jesus and the love of the brethren.[13] These two elements manifest the essentials of the Jesus tradition. With them all else is possible. Without them nothing is possible.

The gospel also deemphasized the ritual of baptism and the eucharist in favor of the faith foundation for these sacraments. Baptism by water makes sense only if the individual has been baptized in faith by the Spirit. The eucharist can be celebrated only if the community first believes in the Lord and has committed itself to Jesus.

Authority exists primarily in the Spirit. In the epilogue, as already noted, the community accepts the apostolic authority of Peter but on the conditions that he love Jesus and die for the sheep.

The church of the community of the beloved disciple emphasizes individual faith, the love of the brethren, and egalitarian spirit with full reign given to freedom, spontaneity and creativity. The weakness of such an approach is evident. The community did not survive in a sinful world. Structure and organization protects and ensures perdurance even though it may also stifle. This community makes its contribution especially in the face of the organization of Matthew and the triumphalism of Luke.

The Pastorals

The church of the 90s produced other approaches to the community which would continue the Jesus tradition. One word will characterize these letters more than any other: structure. Christianity needed structure, and the author of these epistles had a clear plan. Written with the mantle of the authority of Paul, these letters offer a remedy to avoid disintegration. Presbyter-bishops must be appointed in each town. These individuals will guard against false teachers (1 Tim 4:1–2; 2 Tim 3:6; 4:3 Tit 1:10). Previously we have studied the meaning of these church leaders and how they exercised their authority. They provided stability, preserved the authentic teaching of Jesus, and ruled their communities with power. They taught sound doctrine (Tit 2:1) and maintained continuity (2 Tim 3:14). These epistles arose in a moment of crisis as Christianity dealt with encounters with the larger world and settled in for a long wait for the parousia. Unfortunately, the call for control and structure became the norm for most Christian churches. The presbyter-bishops alone teach, alone carry on the tradition, alone provide the vision for the future.

Strong leadership with a central control has worked well in the history of Christianity, especially in Roman Catholic tradition. This facet of the Jesus tradition has shone more brilliantly than others. To some extent, for some Christians this is the only facet of being church. The pastoral epistles offer much that merits acceptance and adoption. They do not, however, offer everything.

This chapter began with a loosely united group of followers of Jesus and concludes with a well-organized hierarchical church. Because this is the conclusion of the first century does not mean necessarily that all has been a positive development leading to this conclusion. Each understanding of how the Christian church may function has its merits. These qualities continue through the centuries. Most of the elements which contemporary believers associate with "church" resulted from the sociological, psychological or anthropological needs of people. Many elements which some may think are of divine origin are in fact of very human origin. As the church continues to develop, the forms of its ministry and structure will develop. Always, however, believers of every time and place will teach and preach, overcome evil and forgive sins. Jesus ministered thus. His church has no choice but to do likewise.

Much of the development that took place in the last third of the first century to the first quarter of the second century remains in shadows.[14] Recently two American scholars have produced a work[15] trying to trace the development in the understanding of Christian ministry in the two ancient capitals of Antioch and Rome. John Meier traced a development in Antioch, beginning with some clues found in Galatians and Acts. He contends that the gospel of Matthew originated in Antioch and that it shows further development in church understanding than previous written documents. He also offers insights into the third generation of Christians as disclosed in the writings of Ignatius of Antioch.[16] Just as tensions existed in the Antiochean church from the time of Peter and Matthew, so it seems that Ignatius inherited dissident groups on the left and on the right. For all the differences, however, between the church of Matthew and the churches associated with Peter, the

Christian community at Antioch at the end of the first century and the beginning of the second was in close continuity with its predecessors in Christian belief. We can speak about the ministry of large Christian centers, but these should always exist in continuity.[17]

Raymond Brown in the same work[18] traces the development of the Roman church from its origins and finds in the epistle to the Romans further insights into the Roman Christian community. He then examines Rome during the period of second generation Christianity as evidenced in the first letter of Peter and the letter to the Hebrews. He discovers aspects of the third generation of Christians in Rome in the writings of Clement of Rome.

The first generation of Christians in Antioch struggled with problems of authority in ministry with various factions of Jewish Christians and Gentile converts. Antioch in the 40s witnessed disputes among the Hellenists and Paul on the one side and Peter and followers of James on the other. These same struggles continued into the 70s with conservative and liberal Jewish Christians contending for authority in ministry with an increasing majority of Gentile Christians. Matthew, as we have already seen, tried to maintain the old as well as introduce the new in his community. He used the authority of Peter as he tried to create a centrist position. At the same time Matthew also knew that authority in the church was also exercised by charismatic leaders, prophets and teachers and attempted, at least in principle, to prevent Christianity from becoming too autocratic. In spite of these reservations, recognized by the author of Matthew, this gospel and his understanding of church order was an important fount from which within two decades of Matthew a firm authoritative structure of single-bishop, presbyters and deacons emerged.[19]

In his treatment of Rome, Brown suggests that the strongest strain of Christianity in Rome came from Jerusalem.

When Paul wrote to Rome seeking support for the church in Jerusalem and also preparing for his own coming to that city, he had moderated his viewpoint toward Judaism.[20] His expression of Christian faith in Rome, as well as his eventual martyrdom there, created a mantle of authority for him. Paul and Peter became pillars of the Roman church, although Peter's influence remained dominant. At the end of the first century, Clement of Rome combined aspects of the imperial authority and order of the city with the religious tradition of Jesus through Peter and Paul. This formed the foundation of the later church development of structure.

Antioch had quickly developed an authority of a single bishop with presbyters and deacons under him. Rome retained much longer the structure of plural presbyter-bishops[21] with deacons under them, but with the Roman understanding of authority the imperial order became associated with church structure. Ignatius of Antioch influenced the church in its ultimate adoption of a threefold order of bishop, presbyters and deacons. Rome's appreciation of fixed order based on apostolic succession, as seen in Clement, gave that structure much of its sacral and sociological import. Thus both Rome and Antioch influenced the authority structure of the early Christian church.[22]

A multiplicity of possible authority structures in the New Testament gradually became narrowed down to an authority that seemed more in accord with an absolute/autocratic structure. Surely the more charismatic type of ministry and the learning of the fathers of the church served well the early development of Christianity, but with the strong influence of Roman imperial systems together with the development of heretical movements in the church the emergence of a strong centralized authority became inevitable. The inclusion of the study of Antioch and Rome in this chapter demonstrates that in the eventual emergence of a single bishop with imperial-type power did not develop out of a vacuum. The seeds for such development may be found in the New Testament itself as well as the interpretation given to the teaching of Jesus by his earliest followers.

Such developments, however, never remain absolute. With changes in society, with demands increasing upon the Christian church to respond to ever-new challenges, forms of ministry will always adapt to current needs. If any absolute exists, it can only be the absolute of Jesus himself who came to serve and to give his life for others. His church can do no less, and thus church members must serve and willingly give of themselves completely in that service.

CHAPTER 7

The Ministry of Jesus and the Church Today

The ministry of Jesus consisted of preaching and teaching, healing, overcoming evil and forgiving sins. He accomplished this ministry as an itinerant preacher in a small geographical area of the world in a very limited time period. While engaged in his ministry he gathered people around him, both men and women. In his lifetime and thereafter, these individuals continued the same ministry, bringing teaching, healing and the forgiveness of sins to all who would respond in faith. Once they experienced the presence of the risen Lord, these same individuals began a ministry that eventually brought Christianity to the center of the world, Rome, and from there it has spread throughout the globe over the past two millennia.

Ministry continues because the authority and power of God continues to inspire and give foundation for Christian activity in every age. Those who profess belief in Jesus as Lord serve each other, even to the point of being willing to die for each other (Jn 10). Joined together by a common faith and supported by a mutual love, these members of the Christian community reach out to others. They invite peoples of every race and tradition to join their numbers. Their ministry, however, goes beyond the confines of their own community to embrace the entire world.

Christian ministry extends to all. Different cultures can find expression in a common Christian faith. Different groups of people, divided in any way, can find a sense of unity by being part of a confessing community. Rich and poor, old and young, geniuses and ordinary people of every race can find fulfillment within the welcoming arms of the Christian community.

Just as Jesus forced no one to accept his teaching, contemporary Christianity continues that same tradition. No constraint joins people to Christianity. With a sense of freedom, individuals join ranks with others of faith. No one ever need feel any sense of force to remain. People must freely come and may freely leave. Otherwise, Christianity fails to follow the example of its founder. Freedom characterized those within the Christian community, and in freedom people chose to join and remain or leave.

The church of Jesus Christ exists as the development of the early Christian ministry. In many ways, to refer to the earliest Christian communities as church is anachronistic. They were not "church" in the way we use the word today. If by "church" we mean a local community of believers united with a common faith, having an autonomy from other local "church" communities, then the word can be used. This, however, is not the ordinary meaning of the word in usage today.

It seems better to use the word church for what eventually developed at the very end of the first century and then began to flourish especially in subsequent centuries. Christianity went from a group of house "churches," each with autonomy, to a worldwide organization. The process was not complete in one generation nor in one century. Much of what we call the church today is the result of development in the middle ages and more recently in the development of mass communication in the last century. The image of a worldwide organization such as the Roman Catholic Church with headquarters in Rome, with Roman congregations for the appointment of bishops and for the regulation of doctrine and sacramental life, with diplomats, and with offices for education and for ecumenical and interfaith relationships, is the church of the twentieth century and not the church of the earliest followers of Jesus. Something similar could be said of other large Christian church organizations in the world today.

However different from those earliest years, the church continues the same ministry of Jesus and his apostles and disciples. The church teaches and preaches; the church overcomes evil in its healing ministry and the church forgives sins. United by a common faith and a willingness to give to each other in service, the believers in the twentieth century do not differ from the believers in the earliest days of Christianity. The world still needs teaching and healing and forgiving. The church community fulfills this ministry with the same power of God and acts on the same authority which founded the ministry of Jesus and his apostles and disciples.

How the ministry continues differs. No one can doubt that any organization which hopes to respond to the needs of a world community needs structure. Early enough those first believers in Jesus recognized a need for organization. The gospel of Matthew, the gospel of Luke and the Acts of the Apostles, and the pastoral epistles all call for some organization. Overseer or elders help the community to survive. Good teaching which gives people a sense of confidence and support for their lives belongs to Christianity as much as the celebration of the eucharist. Leadership with authority and power that orchestrates the teaching and the ministry of contemporary Christianity must characterize a worldwide community.

Organization, however, is not enough. The witness of the community of the beloved disciple alone gives us enough warning about the pitfalls of a hierarchical and organized church. Even Matthew knew of the dangers and built in some governors. Spirit-filled, charismatic, creative and spontaneous people belong in the church with the leaders who base their authority and power on appointment. Christianity needs the "unusual" or even the "strange" people in its midst to call the whole church to repentance. Christianity needs the unlikely prophets who point out the lack of the presence of the divine in contemporary moments. Christianity must cultivate the free-thinkers who call to task the tried and true. Christianity must find room for the marginal and those on the edge who keep the church honest. Only with such can the church continue to fulfill its destiny as continuing the ministry of Jesus. If the despised members of society, the tax collectors, publicans, prostitutes, the sinners and shunned, received a welcome by Jesus and often became leaders of the early Christian community, then today's counterparts belong in this community as well. If Peter and the other closest followers of Jesus who sinned became the pillars of the church, then a life of righteousness is not always the prerequisite for ministry. The two thousand years of Christianity give sufficient witness to such traditions. Augustine was not always the great saint, nor was Ignatius and a host of others. The church needs people who will serve each other by healing, by forgiving and by overcoming evil. Often enough the leaders of the church sinned and they continue to do so. The fate of every human being to sin exists throughout the church, both in the sanctuary and in the pew. The church will always be a sinful church which the Lord loves, and the church will survive as it loves the Lord.[1]

One group in particular served the ministry of Christianity well in these early days and then for centuries lived a life of service deprived of any share in the authority of the church. Women have ministered silently. Now the time has come for women to share in the authority and power of ministry. They are the outcasts who need to be brought in. They are the forgotten who need to be remembered. Women are the marginal, the unlikely, who can bring a new vitality to church authority and power. They can renew the ministry that stands forever in need of renewal.

The church as the people of God, the gathering of the faith community, equalizes and democratizes the whole community. As a people on the move, we have a common lot. All need salvation; all have fallen short; all need to be raised up by a gracious God. All feel the need for the sustaining and supporting presence of the one God. As God's people, the Spirit is promised to all. God alone, and in a sovereign way, directs communication with all. To anyone God may assign any mission and grant an increase of the spirit to fulfill that mission.

Charisms of the spirit appear in everyday life. The Spirit lays open people's hearts, and they respond as teachers, or preachers, or administrators or healers. The one people of God contribute, each in his or her own way, to build up the church. No one can lay claim exclusively to any charism, but each contributes to the whole.

As the body of Christ the church functions with an interlocking of authority and power. Those who have been appointed to function as administrators often function as a hierarchy. The more noble parts of the church as the body of Christ exercise the more important leadership roles in authority and power. They continue the ministry of Jesus, however, in a manner which should always take into consideration the common faith of the people of God.

The contemporary church stands confident in its organization and its sense of Christianity as structured as the body of Christ. Often, however, the church lacks the freely endowed people filled with the Spirit. Somehow all elements must be present if Christianity hopes to remain faithful to its founder.

The understanding of early Christian ministry will not solve all of the problems of the contemporary church, but it will give some direction. More freedom and a willingness to allow for some common ordinary chaos can help much. Everyone may claim to be a centrist, but in fact centrists encourage and support compromises. No one on the left or right can ever be considered a centrist. No extreme should find a permanent enshrinement in the church which lays its foundation on Jesus of Nazareth.

Where we will go in the future depends on where we have been in the past. If nothing more, this book calls for less control. What can be lost? If God is with the church, then all things are possible. If the Spirit guides the whole church, then no one part of the community can ever exclude another part. Wisdom and knowledge and grace flourish in the church of Nepal and Kenya as well as in Miami, New York and Rome. God has begun a good work in Jesus, and in the church of Jesus God alone will bring this good work to a conclusion. Ministry will continue.

APPENDIX

The Petrine Function: The Ministry of the Bishop of Rome

Many Roman Catholics assume that after the death of Peter every bishop of Rome was aware of the special authority which he inherited as the successor of the chief of the apostles. To explain the lack of exercise of such a universal power, apologists replied that the circumstances did not merit any intervention. Often these same apologists still believed, however, that the authority resided in the office of the bishop of Rome, just waiting to come into great prominence.[1]

Contemporary theologians are more aware of the lack of conclusive evidence documenting such an understanding of the role of the bishop of Rome. The earliest fathers of the church cited to support these views, Clement of Rome, Ignatius and Irenaeus, do not offer undisputed evidence and therefore cannot be used without some reservation. To understand the eventual exercise of papal authority we do not need to suppose that the post-apostolic church was immediately in such full possession of itself, and in particular of its structure, that it immediately asserted and exercised a primacy in authority given to the bishop of Rome.[2] Just as we gradually developed an understanding of Jesus as recorded in four gospels and the various other writings of the New Testament, so gradually the church began to understand its own structure and its form of authority.

The need for a central authority became more evident

when divisions in the church and among the bishops made it apparent that a single sign and cause of unity for the universal church could best fulfill the continuation of the mission of the Lord.[3] Gradually the bishop of Rome began to fulfill the ministry similar to that type of ministry which Peter fulfilled in apostolic times. Such an experience caused a rereading of the scriptures in the light of this historical necessity: the church began to see in the bishop of Rome a manifestation of the Petrine function of "strengthening the brethren" (Lk 22:32).

Today most Roman Catholic theologians and historians recognize the interplay between historical factors or anthropological needs as well as the divine commission to preach the gospel to the whole world to explain the origin of papal ministry. Many such factors such as the place of Rome as an imperial city contributed to the development of papal authority. We can conclude that the structure was not instituted by Christ in a direct fashion. What gradually emerged in the church stemming from Christ was guided by the power of the Spirit but also included some elements which are time-conditioned. We may speak of a divine institution but in a carefully nuanced and refined way.[4] This does not imply that the papacy itself is the result of merely historical processes but that these processes were part of the divine plan for the church. Once we are part of the faith community we can recognize in historical and anthropological elements the will of God.[5] For most Roman Catholic theologians the papacy with its full exercise of office shares in the mystery of the church and thus forms an object of faith.[6] The study of the origins of Christian ministry in the New Testament offers a possibility that the office of the pope may itself continue to change. The understanding of the role of authority in ministry in the present world, especially as we see how the historical factors of the history of Christianity have already altered the understanding of authority the papacy, offers possibilities for further changes.

THE LEONINE TRADITION

The reign of the emperor Constantine (285-337) marked the transition of the Christian church from a persecuted people into a legal, corporate personality within the framework of established Roman law. When the Christian church became the official state religion, the leaders of the church assumed a role in the church not unlike the role the emperor had in civil affairs. Thereafter the church took on more of a structure based on the form of the Roman empire. The line between church and state was often transgressed. Christian emperors sometimes treated the church as a department of civil government and church leaders sometimes treated the state as an institution inferior to that of the church. The relationship between the authority of the church and the authority of the state continued to present problems throughout the middle ages and continues to the present day.

As the temporal power of the empire declined, many governmental functions of administration and protection devolved upon the office of bishop and, in particular, the bishop of Rome. Bishops became prince-bishops and had both a civil and ecclesiastical authority. Leo the Great, the bishop of Rome, went out from Rome to meet Attila the Hun and protected the city and its population. Theologians agree that this same pope formulated the doctrine of papal primacy and authority that had been present in seminal forms for the previous two centuries. Leo clearly formulated his belief on the relationship between Jesus and Peter and then Peter and the bishop of Rome. These views founded the western understanding of the role and office of the bishop of Rome as an office of primacy in authority.[7]

Of particular interest are the arguments that Leo used in describing the authority of the bishop of Rome. He was trained in Roman law and explained succession through the use of the legal concept of heredity. In Roman law the heir had the same rights, authority and obligations as the one he replaced.[8] Thus the pope could exercise the same authority and power that Christ had entrusted to Peter. Leo's interpretation of Matthew 16:18–19 demonstrated that he believed the authority of Peter over the apostles was a sharing in the absolute authority of Jesus himself.[9]

To the idea of juridical continuity taken from Roman law Leo added his understanding of a mystical or sacramental continuity: "Peter in heaven continues to govern the church through his heir and vicar, and in this sense the pope is Peter himself mystically continuing to exercise his authority in human history."[10]

As an aside important for our understanding of the exercise of ministry in the church, this same period saw the rise of monasticism. In this new form of Christian life a spiritual and charismatic type of ministry could continue to function. Monks enjoyed an independent type of authority often in opposition to what had come to be seen as the hierarchical and juridical authority. Such an understanding of this more freely creative ministry was more prevalent in the east and indeed continues to exist in the eastern church. In the eighth century, especially after the monothelite and iconoclastic controversies in the east, the monks assumed more of the role of authority figures as "men of God" and exercised their power outside the normal channels of church life. In the west a similar development occurred as abbots and monks created their own sphere of influence.

Such a development did not create a total opposition between the authority as exercised by bishops and pope and that exercised by holy men and women, since often enough the bishops themselves were chosen from the ranks of the monastic clergy. But what did develop was an understanding of authority associated with office, unlike the New Testament ideas of ministry concerned fundamentally with service and functioning more charismatically than institutionally and hierarchically.

THE MIDDLE AGES

Although Leo's teaching on the papacy continued to dominate Roman Catholic theology up to the present time, not every member of the church adopted the teaching nor was it accepted everywhere in Christianity. Several centuries passed before Leo's theory became practice. Even the title "Papa," a word used earlier for all bishops, did not become reserved for the bishop of Rome until the sixth century, and then only in the west. Gregory VII still had to assert in 1075 that only one pope existed in the world.[11] To understand this development, however, demands more background in the history of the church which is beyond the scope of this book.

VATICAN II

Prior to the Second Vatican Council the authority and power of the bishop of Rome was interpreted in the same manner as throughout the early and later middle ages: Christ promised and conferred an absolute authority upon Peter; this primacy in authority continued in the church and can be found in the exercise of the authority of the bishop of Rome. This recent council did not alter the notion of supreme authority of pope and bishops over the church but did claim that this authority is to be exercised as service and in a collegial way.[12] Pope and bishops will use their authority and power but only to build up the flock.[13] The church has developed in its understanding of authority but ultimately has returned to the notion of authority as service as witnessed in the New Testament.

The authority of the papacy for most Roman Catholics symbolizes the authority of the church. Even for Protestants the popes of recent times have exercised authority not only within the Roman tradition but also beyond the confines of the Catholic Church. The pope has become an authority figure for Christianity even if some aspects of Christianity have problems with certain elements of the papal authority structure. Certainly the life of the Christian, Roman Catholic or not, should not be centered upon the pope, but his presence within the Roman Catholic community and his influence outside this community, both in religious and world affairs, necessitates a study of his role in the past and the present with some forward look to what a renewed papacy would mean for the Christian church.

In an age of revisionism and in a book that purports to deal with an analysis of ministry within the context of the New Testament, the ministry of the bishop of Rome may be examined with whatever changes necessary becoming part of the changing church. Some Roman Catholics may see any attempt to limit or reevaluate the ministry and function of the pope as traitorous to their tradition, but for many other Roman Catholics a renewal of the church based upon the return to the biblical traditions as sanctioned by the Second Vatican Council includes a rethinking and restructuring of the office of the bishop of Rome. The historical development may have created the need for an absolute type of authority and a power that is often nutrient at its best. But can such an understanding of authority and power continue in the future, especially in the light of the understanding of ministry in the New Testament?

The First Vatican Council defined that the papacy is of divine institution, that the pope enjoys a primacy of jurisdiction over all particular churches, pastors, and believers, and that when he speaks *ex cathedra* as successor of Peter he is blessed with infallibility. This council appears authoritarian especially when we compare it with the documents from the Second Vatican Council. This more recent gathering of the bishops of the Roman Church manifests an openness, a return to a biblical tradition, a concern for pluralism and adaptability, a suggestion that the Holy Spirit operates throughout the church and not just through the authoritative pronouncements of popes and bishops. This same council often seems to substitute an attitude of service, self-criticism, adaptability and friendliness to the strong defensive and authoritarian attitude of the First Vatican Council.

As a result of this change in attitude many Catholics see a need for a revision of papal authority and an examination of its use of power:

> In the present age of revisionism, the papacy, like many other Catholic symbols, has become a sign of contradiction. Some Catholics strongly committed to the specifics of their own tradition, look upon the pope as the guardian and cornerstone of faith. To them, any questioning or limitation of papal authority is treasonous; it plays into the hands of the enemy and damages the Catholic cause. Others, committed to a thoroughgoing renewal of the church, hold that for the effectiveness of renewal it is essential that the papacy be rethought and restructured.[14]

The study of the New Testament roots of episcopal authority and the gradual emergence of this office in the church implies that we should not speak of the divine institution of the papacy as a simply accepted fact dependent upon the expressed will of the Lord. We can speak of the divine institution only in the context of historical needs for the Christian church. Rather than speak of divine institution[15] we might speak of the Petrine office, ministry or function within the church.[16] In theory most will accept the need for this ministry to continue to exist within the church, but how it is exercised could be further adapted based upon the historical needs of the church. A single individual could continue this office, or it could be done by a group of individuals with a possible division of powers: judicial, legislative and administrative:

> In theory, the Petrine function could be performed either by a single individual presiding over the whole Church or by some kind of committee, board, synod, or parliament—possibly with a "division of power" into judicial, legislative, administrative, and the like.[17]

Since both Vatican Councils left unanswered the proper relationship between the pope and the universal episcopacy and ecumenical councils, further discussion within the Roman tradition seems necessary, and this discussion need not be locked into the authority structures of the past provided the function of Peter continues in the church.

The change in geopolitical realities in the past thirty years also calls for an examination of the operations of the papacy. In theory the pope has supreme control over all of the agencies, secretariats, and congregations, but as is true with all bureaucracy, they tend to have a life of their own apart from the pope who bears ultimate authority and responsibility. It is an example of authority without power. With the pope spending more time outside of the Vatican, a division of power and authority seems inevitable if the church does not wish the bureaucracy to move into a vacuum created by other circumstances.

The decision at Vatican I to avoid a declaration stating that the primacy of Peter is irrevocably attached to the see of Rome leaves open to question whether the primate of the Roman Catholic Church someday will be other than the bishop of Rome. We could even envision an authority structure by which the primacy would rotate among several sees:

In principle, therefore, it remains open to discussion whether someone other than the bishop of Rome might someday be the primate of the Catholic Church. It would be conceivable, for example, that the bishop of another city might hold the primacy, or that the papacy might rotate among several sees, somewhat as the presidency of the Security Council in the United Nations rotates among representatives of various nations.[18]

The institutionalization of this Petrine function seems paramount. Only then can the church have an effective sign and cause of unity. Having any individual to fulfill this function strongly symbolizes this unity, but whether this is the only possibility for the future should not be accepted as a given.

A more thorny problem, especially in the light of the New Testament, is the question of the authority and jurisdiction of the pope. I say authority and jurisdiction, since for many these are equated. They fail to see that authority can exist and need not be seen in terms of jurisdiction. According to the First Vatican Council the pope as successor of Peter exercises a jurisdiction that is universal, ordinary, immediate, truly episcopal, supreme and full.[19] Jurisdiction is a legal term derived from a judicial tradition. With the development of papal authority the pope took on many features of a political power unlike the ideas we have seen in the development of the New Testament. This jurisdiction of Rome differed considerably in the history of Christianity. In the early centuries Rome functioned with strict authority and power over the bishops of Italy, and in the rest of the west he intervened only in special cases. The eastern churches had their own authority figures who eventually became the patriarchs. The churches outside of the Roman empire had little relationship to the bishop of Rome.

In the middle ages the church of Rome took on a more universal jurisdiction. Thomas Aquinas in the thirteenth century and Francesco Suarez in the sixteenth century regarded the church as a strict monarchy in which all of the bishops depended upon the pope for their own jurisdiction. The term jurisdiction is not the most felicitous, since it seems to juridicize the authority of Peter. The New Testament does not give to Peter alone the authority and power to make laws, and without this authority the meaning of jurisdiction has little significance.

The fathers of the First Vatican Council debated the concept of jurisdiction, intending to avoid a strictly legal interpretation. Federico Zinelli contended that the term episcopal should make it clear that the pope exercises authority as a pastor:

> Bishop Federico Zinelli, the official reporter for chapter 3 of *Pastor Aeternus,* made the point that the meaning of the term "jurisdiction" in this chapter is qualified by its adjectival modifiers. In particular, he contended, the term "episcopal" should make it clear that the pope's authority is that of a pastor, whose mission it is to feed the flocks entrusted to his care. Just as individual bishops are missioned to feed the particular flocks committed to them, so Zinelli argued, the pope is commissioned to pasture the whole flock of Christ.[20]

The pope then should not be seen as a universal ruler with an absolute type of authority but an authority modeled on that of the earliest followers of Jesus who in turn modeled their authority on the service of Jesus himself. The authority given to Peter as attested in the New Testament should not be seen as primarily jurisdictional, nor can it be seen as merely honorary. A better designation would be sacramental.

> . . . some Catholics continue to question the appropriateness of the term "jurisdiction" as applied to the kind of

authority that the pope should have over other bishops. As Cornelius Ernst points out, Vatican I posed the question in terms of an opposition between two types of primacy—honor and jurisdiction—so that the term "jurisdiction" was used to exclude a mere primacy of honor (C. Ernst, "The Primacy of Peter: Theology and Ideology," *New Blackfriars,* 50 (1969), 347–55, 399–404). Seen from the perspective of our own day, this dichotomy is unsatisfactory. The authority of Jesus, which according to Matthew 16:17–19 was in some sort transmitted to Peter, cannot be suitably called either honorary or jurisdictional. There is a third kind of primacy, properly theological in nature, to which Ernst gives the name ontological or, in a wide sense, sacramental. In the writings of Leo the Great, he maintains, sacramental themes of primacy predominate over the juridical themes that later became so prominent. In a sacramental view of primacy, the notion of papal power moves away from jurisdiction in the legal sense toward a style of leadership based on charism and moral authority.[21]

A sacramental type of authority lends itself to a leadership style based on charism and moral authority instead of a legal and absolute authority.

We can still accept a "primacy of honor" provided that we recognize that all honor in the church rests upon service:

> Some careful scholars since Vatican II maintain that the notion of a "primacy of honor" is capable of being defended, even from within the Roman Catholic tradition. The pope, like a patriarch, is not a superbishop; he is a bishop among bishops. He exercises a primacy not over bishops but rather among bishops and is, in that sense, a first among equals. He may be said to have a primacy of honor, provided it be recognized, as Père Duprey reminds us, that there is no honor in the church except in view of a service.[22]

This special service given to the pope has been explained in the Second Vatican Council as the authority "to preside over the assembly of charity,"[23] to foster collegial relationships among the regional bishops and the particular churches. Ultimately we may move into an authority that is sometimes charismatic; other times the ministry will rest on learning, and occasionally this authority might be exercised as legal or bureaucratic, but the absolute type of authority should recede along with the claim to a legal authority to allow charismatic authority and the authority of learning to become paramount.

Frequently in the history of Christianity the eastern churches and the Protestant churches as well have bristled with the insistence by the Roman church on jurisdiction. The ideas as presented above would help considerably to assuage some of these historical fears. The concept of papal primacy could be interpreted more in accord with the ideas from the New Testament, less legalistically and more in accord with the collegial and conciliar view of the church.

Many of the ideas of ministry and authority as presented in the initial chapters of this book will influence the understanding of the exercise of ministry and authority by the bishop of Rome. We may readily accept the charismatic type of authority if the person who occupies the throne of Peter possesses such a charism. Unfortunately, although the office of bishop of Rome depends upon a charism, not every occupant of the throne of Peter possessed charismatic authority. Inevitably the one who exercises the function of Peter will have to base his responsibility more on learning and bureaucratic/legalistic types of authority than that of the absolute type. With regard to power, the ultimate expectation would be the exercise of an integrative and persuasive power, although at times the true pastor and teacher will also exercise a nutrient power.

Notes

CHAPTER 1

1. *Church Dogmatics* (Minneapolis: Eerdmans, 1900), IV/1, 297ff.
2. John F. O'Grady, "Authority and Power: Issues for the Contemporary Church", *Louvain Studies*, Fall 1984, 122–140.
3. The root is *auctor*, referring to "he who brings about the existence of any object. Cf. *A Latin Dictionary*, Lewis and Short, 1955.
4. I emphasize influence since this takes into account the rights and dignity of the other. I wish to avoid the behavioralist approach particularly espoused by B. F. Skinner, *Beyond Freedom and Dignity* (New York: Vintage, 1972).
5. The root is the word *possum*, meaning an ability, or the power of doing something. Cf. Lewis and Short.
6. Cf. Martin Hengel, *The Charismatic Leader and His Followers* (New York: Crossroad, 1981). The subject of the article is Jesus. For further ideas see J. F. O'Grady, "Jesus, His Authority, Power and Leadership," *Studies in Formative Spirituality*, Vol. 23 (1982).
7. All of these designations come from Rollo May, *Power and Innocence* (New York: Norton, 1972), 99–104. May proposes that manipulative power is an example of operant conditioning based upon anxiety. I am inclined to see more positive value in manipulative power, at least theoretically. This will become more evident as I use these ideas in examining the ministry of Jesus.

CHAPTER 2

1. Cf. R. Brown, *The Virginal Conception and the Bodily Resurrection of Jesus* (New York: Paulist, 1973); "Gospel Infancy Narrative Research 1976–1986," *Catholic Biblical Quarterly* Part I and II, Vol. 38 (1986), 468–483, 660–680.

2. Cf. ibid.; P. Perkins, *The Resurrection* (New York: Doubleday, 1984).

3. Cf. R. Fuller, "Pre-existence Christology: Can We Dispense with It?" *Word and World,* Vol. 2 (1982) 29–33.

4. We shall discuss this in detail in a later chapter.

5. Cf. R. Brown, *The Birth of the Messiah* (New York: Doubleday, 1977) 29–30; "Gospel Infancy Narrative Research," 679.

6. Cf. O. Cullmann, "Functional Christology," *Theology Digest,* Vol. 10, 1962, 215–219; L. Malevez, "Functional Christology in the New Testament," *Theology Digest,* Vol. 10, 1962, 77–83.

7. Scholars generally agree that Paul is quoting a hymn which arose in another context to address another problem. Cf. J. Sanders, *New Testament Christological Hymns* (Cambridge: The University Press, 1971).

8. The most complete scholarly and thorough study of both Matthew and Luke is R. Brown's *The Birth of the Messiah.*

9. Cf. *ibid.* 292–297.

10. Cf. *ibid.* 298–303. See also: J. Fitzmyer, *The Gospel According to Luke I–IX* (New York: Doubleday, 1982) 337–338. Fitzmyer agrees with Brown that the step-parallelism in the two announcements of the births of John and Jesus demands that the birth of Jesus involve a more extraordinary conception. Luke's words, however, in and of themselves, without the influence from the thought of Matthew where the virginal conception is clearly formulated, can be interpreted to mean that Jesus was born in an ordinary human way.

11. Today, few if any scholars accept the notion that Mary herself contributed to the origin of the birth narratives in the gospels, in particular the gospel of Luke. Both Luke and Matthew use Old Testament material and develop their stories for theological reasons to suit the needs of their community. One possible historical catalyst for the idea of a virginal conception was the remembrance that Jesus was born unduly early after his parents had come to live together. R. Brown presents a full analysis of this theory in his work *The Birth of the Messiah,* 517–542.

12. Certain theologians interpret the virginal conception as theological and will not accept its historicity. Among Roman Catholics such is the opinion of J. L. MacKenzie and M. Hellwig. They come

to their conclusions from different perspectives but each will agree on the symbolic significance of the virginal conception. R. Brown in two articles summarized the thought on the infancy nartratives since the publication of his book *The Virginal Conception.* Cf. "Gospel Infancy Narrative Research from 1976 to 1986": Part I (Matthew); Part II (Luke), *The Catholic Biblical Quarterly,* Vol. 48 (1986) 468–483, 660–680. Brown presents a complete picture of the various theories with regard to the question of historicity. Since this present work is not primarily concerned with the question of historicity but with the meaning of these narratives as coming from a church community, further information may be found in this article and in the references cited by Brown.

13. R. Brown, *The Virginal Conception and the Bodily Resurrection of Jesus,* 66.

CHAPTER 3

1. Cf. Gerald O'Collins, *Interpreting the Resurrection* (New York: Paulist, 1988). See also O'Collins, *Jesus Risen* (New York: Paulist, 1987). The former deals with some of the historical questions; the latter includes much of the theological perspective.

2. Cf. Jerome Neyrey, *The Resurrection* (Wilmington: Glazier, 1988). I am particularly indebted to this author which will become evident in the unfolding of this chapter.

3. The material available on ministry continues to increase. The general works—B. Cooke, *Ministry to Word and Sacraments* (Philadelphia: Fortress, 1975); T. O'Meara, *Theology of Ministry* (New York: Paulist, 1983); E. Schillebeeckx, *Ministry: Leadership in the Community of Jesus Christ* (New York: Crossroad, 1981)—offer much information on the New Testament as well as some historical and theological developments.

4. Cf. Neyrey, 9–11.

5. I prefer the understanding of "mystery" as explained by K. Rahner: knowing something but never knowing everything. Cf. K. Rahner, "The Concept of Mystery in Catholic Theology," in *Theological Investigations,* Vol. 4 (Baltimore: Helicon, 1966) 36–76.

6. Cf. R. Brown, *The Virginal Conception and the Bodily Resurrection of Jesus* (New York: Paulist, 1973) 100.

7. *Ibid.* 117–125.

8. The question arises: Where did the original pre-Pauline formula begin and end? It seems that the transmitted tradition consisted of: "that Christ died . . . was buried, and that he was raised and that he appeared." Cf. Brown, 82

9. Cf. G. O'Collins, "Is the Resurrection an Historical Event?" *Heythrop Journal,* Vol. 8, 1967, 381–387.

10. Cf. R. Fuller, *The Formation of the Resurrection Narratives* (New York: Macmillan, 1971) 23–27.

11. All of the exegetes make reference to the use of this word. Cf. Brown, 90; Fuller, 27–35. This last author gives an extensive treatment of the word.

12. Cf. Fuller, 32–33

13. Cf. Neyrey, 17.

14. Cf. Fuller, 36–38.

15. *Ibid.* 42–49.

16. Cf. Neyrey, 18–21.

17. *Ibid.* 23–24.

18. Cf. Brown, 100–118. The author offers charts to explain the variant gospel narratives with regard to both the appearances and the visit to the tomb.

19. Cf. J. F. O'Grady, "The Role of the Beloved Disciple," *Biblical Theology Bulletin,* Vol. 9 (1979).

20. Cf. O'Collins, *Jesus Risen,* 119–121.

21. Cf. Neyrey, 27–28.

22. *Ibid.* 34–37.

23. For a fuller explanation of these terms, see Neyrey, 36. I am particularly indebted to this author for his insights into leadership in ministry as exemplified in the resurrection appearances.

24. For a fuller explanation of this commissioning see John Meier, *Matthew* (Wilmington: Glazier, 1980) 366–374.

25. A complete study of this episode is provided by R. Dillon, *From Eye Witnesses to Ministers of the Word; Tradition and Composition in Luke 24* (Rome: Biblical Institute Press, 1978).

26. Cf. Neyrey, 50–60.

27. Cf. R. Brown, *The Gospel of John, XII-XXI* (New York: Doubleday, 1970), 965–1017; *The Community of the Beloved Disciple* (New York: Paulist, 1979) 183–198. In the latter article Brown gives important insights into the role of women in the fourth gospel.

28. Cf. Brown, *The Community of the Beloved Disciple,* 187–191; Neyrey, 72–73.

29. Here I am following the suggestion by Neyrey, 76–78.

30. Cf. J. F. O'Grady, *The Four Gospels and the Jesus Tradition* (New York: Paulist, 1989) 148–151; J. F. O'Grady, *The Gospel of John* (New York: Pueblo, 1970) 90–91. R. Brown, *The Community of the Beloved Disciple,* 31–34.

31. Cf. Neyrey, 61–75.

32. Cf. R. Schnackenburg, *The Gospel according to St. John* (New York: Crossroad, 1982) 349–351.

33. Cf. J. F. O'Grady, "The Role of the Beloved Disciple."

34. The word "twelve" is used only in two episodes: 6:67–70 in the context of "going away" and the "betrayal," and finally in 20:24, the reference to Thomas, "one of the twelve."

35. Cf. O'Grady, "The Role of the Beloved Disciple"; Neyrey, 84–97.

36. Cf. Brown, *The Community of the Beloved Disciple,* 147–161.

37. Is the resurrection an historical event or not? Much depends on what "historical" means. If the historian deals with time and space, then the resurrection is trans-historical, or meta-historical, for in the resurrection Jesus passes beyond time and space. There were no witnesses to the resurrection. Just as the conception of Jesus had no earthly verification, so his glorification in the resurrection has no earthly verification.

The tomb of Jesus was not part of the eschatological event. Of itself, the empty tomb was probably not at first a sign of the resurrection, and the emptiness of the tomb was probably not formally part of Christian faith in the risen Lord. Christians believe in the risen Lord, not in an empty tomb. We can also say that in all probability the insights into faith shaped the narratives of the discovery of the empty tomb. See R. Brown, *The Virginal Conception and the Bodily Resurrection of Jesus.*

CHAPTER 4

1. Cf. W. Foerster, "Exousia," *Theological Dictionary of the New Testament,* Vol. III (Grand Rapids: Eerdmans, 1964) 562; also O. Betz, "exousia," *Dictionary of the New Testament,* Vol. 2 (Grand Rapids: Zondervan, 1976) 606–611; N. Nash, *Voices of Authority* (London: Patmos, 1976) 20ff.

2. Cf. Foerster, 560ff.

3. *Ibid.* 562.

4. *Antiquities* (Cambridge: Harvard University Press, 1961) 14:302; 20:193; 4:247; 5:109, etc. See Foerster, 564.

5. *Spec. Leg.* 111 (Cambridge: Harvard University Press, 1956) 563. See Foerster, 564.

6. Tob 7:10. In later writings, especially Daniel and Maccabees, the word denotes the power of the king or of God, the power which decides in other authoritarian relationships in life, and thus the authorities.

7. Cf. Foerster, 566ff.

8. *Ibid.* 568. It is his own authority in free agreement with the Father.

9. We have already dealt with this epilogue in the previous chapter. In addition to the cited works, see also J. F. O'Grady, "Johannine Ecclesiology: A Critical Analysis," *Biblical Theology Bulletin,* Vol. 6 (1976). John also implies a power to forgive sins in 20:22–23. As we noted previously, this is given to the disciples. In this gospel the forgiveness of sins is not joined exclusively with the ministry of Peter or the twelve.

10. Cf. W. Grundmann, "Dynamai," *Theological Dictionary of the New Testament,* Vol. III (Grand Rapids: Eerdmans, 1964) 284–317; also O. Betz, "Dynamis," *Dictionary of the New Testament,* Vol. III (Grand Rapids: Zondervan, 1976) 601–606.

11. *Ibid.* 285.

12. Human powers are one part of the cosmic powers. Animals, plants, etc., also have their powers. Cf. Grundmann, 285.

13. *Ibid.*

14. *Ibid.* 286.

15. Cf. B. Kaye and John Rogerson, *Miracles and Mysteries in the Bible* (Philadelphia: Westminster, 1977) 69–83.

16. Cf. Grundmann, 301.

17. Cf. Morton Smith, *Jesus the Magician* (New York: Harper and Row, 1978).

18. We have used these terms in a previous chapter. Authority can be absolute or autocratic, legal and bureaucratic, the authority of learning, and charismatic. See also N. Lash, chapters 2 and 3.

19. We have also referred to exploitative, manipulative, competitive, nutrient and integrative power in a previous chapter.

20. Cf. J. Lambrecht, *Once More Astonished* (New York: Crossroad, 1981) 1–18. Also J. Crossan, *In Parables: The Challenge of the Historical Jesus* (New York: Harper and Row, 1973); J. F. O'Grady, *The Four Gospels and the Jesus Tradition,* 188–195.

CHAPTER 5

1. Cf. A. Richardson, *An Introduction to the Theology of the New Testament* (London: SCM Press, 1958) 312.

2. Cf. R. Brown, *Priest and Bishop* (New York: Paulist, 1970); "Episkope and Episkopos: The New Testament Evidence," *Theological Studies,* Vol. 4 (1980) 322–388.

3. Cf. E. Schweitzer, *Mark.*

4. Cf. J. Fitzmyer, *The Gospel according to Luke* (New York: Doubleday).

5. Cf. Brown, *Priest and Bishop,* 47ff.

6. Cf. S. Kealy, *The Gospel of Luke* (Denville: Dimension, 1979) 414–416; also cf. Brown's analysis of the place of the twelve in the Acts of the Apostles in *Priest and Bishop,* 56–59.

7. Cf. E. Schweizer, *The Good News according to Matthew* (Atlanta: John Knox, 1975) 371; R. Gundry, *Matthew* (Grand Rapids: Eerdmans, 1982) 368–369; J. Meier and R. Brown, *Antioch and Rome* (New York: Paulist: 1983) 64–70.

8. Cf. J. F. O'Grady, *The Four Gospels and the Jesus Tradition,* 155–160.

9. We will treat this chapter in greater detail in a later chapter of this book.

10. Cf. Meier, 70.

11. Cf. L. Sabourin, "La Remission des peches dans Ecriture

Sainte et practique ecclesiale," *Science et Esprit,* Vol. 32 (1980) 299; *Theology Digest,* Vol. 29 (1981); Richardson, 317–319.

12. Cf. R. Schnackenburg, *The Gospel According to St. John,* 326–327: O'Grady, *The Gospel of John,* 90–91.

13. Cf. Brown, "Episkope and Episkopos," 323.

14. Cf. K. Rengstorf, "Apostolos," *Theological Dictionary of the New Testament,* Vol. 1 (Grand Rapids: Eerdmans, 1964) 398–445.

15. Cf. Brown, "Episkope and Episkopos," 328; Richardson, 319.

16. Cf. Brown, *Priest and Bishop,* 73–81.

17. Cf. *Apostolos,* in Kittel, *Theological Dictionary of the New Testament,* 407–445.

18. Cf. Rengstorf, 414; Richardson, 324.

19. Some have attempted to use the studies of Rengstorf to support apostolic succession. Cf. Dom Gregory Dix, *The Apostolic Ministry* (London: 1946). Compare these ideas with Brown, *Priest and Bishop.*

20. Cf. R. Brown, K. Donfried and J. Reumann, *Peter in the New Testament* (New York: Paulist, 1973).

21. For an interesting explanation to the origin of this section of Matthew, see Augustine Stock, "Is Matthew's Presentation of Peter Ironic?" *Biblical Theology Bulletin,* Vol. 17 (1987) 64–69.

22. I believe that Matthew used Peter as an example of a centrist approach to Christianity. See: O'Grady, *The Four Gospels and the Jesus Tradition,* 155–156.

23. Cf. Brown, *Peter in the New Testament,* 83–101.

24. *Ibid.* 119–125.

25. Cf. Schnackenburg, 375–388.

26. Cf. O'Grady, "The Role of the Beloved Disciple," 62. Also cf. P. Le Fort, *Les Structures de l'eglise militante selon s. Jean* (Geneva, 1970).

27. Cf. B. Holmberg, *Paul and Power* (Philadelphia: Fortress, 1978).

28. We will return to this in the next chapter when we deal with some of the churches the apostles left behind.

29. For an interesting insight into the situation in Jerusalem, see P. Achtemeier, *The Quest for Unity in the New Testament* (Philadelphia: Fortress, 1987).

30. Holmberg, 183.

31. *Ibid.* 80ff.

32. Cf. Schnackenburg, 375ff.

33. *Ibid.* 385.

34. Cf. J. F. O'Grady, "The Good Shepherd and the Vine and the Branches," *Biblical Theology Bulletin,* Vol. 8 (1978) 86–89.

35. Cf. Schnackenburg, 142ff.

36. Some manuscripts have an aorist tense; others have a present tense. The difference has caused some scholars to see the gospel as a missionary document, "in order that you may come to believe." The majority of exegetes hold that 20:31 is formulated for those who already believe. Cf. Schnackenburg, 338.

37. *Ibid.* 341–374; Brown, "Episkope and Episkopos," 337; S. Marrow, *John 21, An Essay in Johannine Ecclesiology* (Rome, 1968). Morrow offers the thesis that the final chapter was written with an ecclesial tone to make explicit the ecclesial thought implicit in the body of the gospel. This writer sees the final chapter as the result of the death of the beloved disciple and the need for the community to come to grips with other expressions of ministry in the early church.

38. Cf. Brown, *Priest and Bishop;* Richardson, 325.

39. Brown, "Episkope and Episkopos," 333–334.

40. *Ibid.* 335–337.

41. One group that seems to have suffered most historically in a loss of authority and power were women. In the early church they seemed to have functioned in many ways in a similar manner to men. This changed with the further development of Christianity. Cf. E. Schüssler-Fiorenza, *In Memory of Her* (New York: Crossroad, 1985), chapters 5 and 8. We shall return to this topic in the concluding chapter.

CHAPTER 6

1. Cf. W. Meeks, *The First Urban Christians* (New Haven: Yale University Press, 1983); E. Schillebeeckx, *The Church with a Human Face* (New York: Crossroad, 1987); R. Brown, *The Churches the Apostles Left Behind* (New York: Paulist, 1984).

2. Cf. Schillebeeckx, *The Church with a Human Face,* 41.

3. Cf. Kittel, *Theological* . . . Vol. III, 513.

4. *Ibid.* 502–512.

5. Cf. Schillebeeckx, *The Church with a Human Face,* 46.

6. Cf. P. Achtemeier, *The Quest for Unity in the New Testament* (Philadelphia: Fortress, 1987).

7. Cf. Raymond Brown and John Meier, *Antioch and Rome.*

8. Cf. J. O'Grady, *The Four Gospels and the Jesus Tradition* (New York: Paulist, 1989).

9. Cf. J. Meier, *Antioch and Rome,* 39–44.

10. Cf. Brown, *The Churches the Apostles Left Behind,* 132–134.

11. Cf. Brown, *The Churches the Apostles Left Behind,* 139–145.

12. *Ibid.* 144.

13. Cf. J. O'Grady, "The Good Shepherd and the Vine and the Branches," *Biblical Theology Bulletin.* Vol. 17 (1978).

14. Cf. Meeks, *The First Urban Christians,* for some efforts to explain some of the development based on sociological findings.

15. R. Brown and J. Meier, *Antioch and Rome.*

16. *Ibid.* 11–86.

17. *Ibid.* 85–86.

18. *Ibid.* 87–210.

19. Cf. A. Lemaire, *Les Ministeres aux origines de l'eglise* (Paris: Du Cerf, 1971), 163–168.

20. Cf. Achtemeier, *The Quest for Unity in the New Testament.*

21. Brown and Meier, 163–164.

22. *Ibid.* 213.

CHAPTER 7

1. Cf. K. Rahner, "The Church of Sinners," *Theological Investigations,* Vol. VI (Baltimore: Helicon, 1969) 253–270. "And at the end the Lord will be alone with the woman. And then he will stand erect and look upon this prostitute, his bride, and ask her, 'Woman, where are your accusers? Has no one condemned you?' And she will answer with inexpressible repentance and humility, 'No one, Lord.' And she will be astonished and almost dismayed that no one has done so. But the Lord will come close to her and say, 'Then neither shall I con-

demn you.' He will kiss her forehead and murmur, 'My bride, holy church' " (p. 269).

APPENDIX

1. Cf. M. Miller, *What Are They Saying about Papal Authority?* (New York: Paulist, 1983) 36–37.

2. Cf. P. Granfield, *The Papacy in Transition* (New York: Doubleday, 1980).

3. Cf. J. McCue, "The Roman Primacy in the Second Century and the Development of Dogma," *Theological Studies,* Vol. 25 (1964) 161.

4. *Ibid.* Also cf. A. Dulles, "Papal Authority in Roman Catholicism," in *A Pope for All Christians.* ed. P. McCord (New York: Paulist, 1976) 53.

5. Cf. Brown, *Priest and Bishop, 73.* Also cf. R. Brown, *Biblical Reflections on Crises facing the Church* (New York: Paulist, 1975).

6. A. Dulles, "Jus Divinum as an Ecumenical Problem," *Theological Studies,* Vol. 38 (1977) 695.

7. Cf. W. Ullmann, "Leo I and the Theme of Papal Primacy," *Journal of Theological Studies,* Vol. II (1960).

8. *Ibid.* 33–35.

9. Leo, I, *Sermon,* 3,3.

10. *Ibid.* 3,2.

11. Cf. R. McBrien, *Catholicism* (Oak Grove: Winston Press, 1980) 823.

12. Cf. *Dogmatic Constitution on the Church* #18.

13. *Ibid.* #27.

14. A. Dulles, "Toward a Renewed Papacy," in *The Resilient Chruch* (New York: Doubleday, 1977) 131–132.

15. Cf. C. Peter, "Dimensions of 'Jus Divinum' in Roman Catholic Theology," *Theological Studies,* Vol. 34 (1973) 227–250.

16. Cf. R. Pesch, "The Position and Significance of Peter in the Church of the New Testament," in H. Kung, *Papal Ministry in the Church* (New York: Herder and Herder, 1971) 21–35. Also cf. Brown, *Peter in the New Testament.*

17. Cf. Dulles, "Toward a Renewed Papacy," 127ff.

18. *Ibid.*

19. *The Teaching of the Catholic Church* (Cork: Mercier Press, 1966) 379.

20. Cf. Dulles, "Toward a Renewed Papacy," 122.

21. *Ibid.* 123.

22. *Ibid.* Also cf. P. Duprey, "Brief Reflections on the Title 'Primus inter Pares,' " *One in Christ,* Vol. 10 (1974) 7–12.

23. *Dogmatic Constitution on the Church* #13.